WALTER RODNEY SPEAKS
The Making of an African Intellectual

With an Introduction by
Robert Hill

Foreword by
Howard Dodson

Africa World Press, Inc.

P.O. Box 1892
Trenton, New Jersey 08607

Africa World Press
P.O. Box 1892
Trenton, NJ 08607

© Institute of the Black World 1990

Cover design by Ife Nii Owoo

Typesetting by TypeHouse of Pennington, Inc.

Library of Congress Catalog Card Number: 87-72611

ISBN: 0-86543-071-3   cloth
        0-86543-071-1   paper

CONTENTS

WALTER RODNEY: A BRIEF BIOGRAPHY

Walter Rodney, son of a tailor, was born on March 23, 1942. Ironically, he was murdered on June 13, 1980, not very far from Bent Street in Georgetown, Guyana, where he was born and where he spent his childhood. After attending primary school, he won an open exhibition scholarship to attend Queens College. In doing so, he was to blaze a trail as one of the the early working-class beneficiaries of concessions made in the field of education by the ruling class in Guyana to the fervor of nationalism which was sweeping the country in the 1950s. While at Queens he excelled academically, as well as in the field of athletics.

In 1960 he won an open scholarship to further his studies at the University of the West Indies in Jamaica. Rodney graduated with a first-class honors degree in history. From U.W.I. he won an open scholarship to the School of Oriental and African Studies in London. At the age of 24 he was awarded a Ph.D. with honors.

In 1970 his Ph.D. dissertation was published by Oxford University Press under the title, *A History of the Upper Guinea Coast, 1545-1800*. This book challenged the assumptions of western historians about African history.

While studying and living in London, Walter found time to participate in discussion circles, speak at Hyde Park and, among other activities, participate in the Symposium on Guyana held at the West Indian Students' Centre, in 1965.

Rodney left London in 1966 to take up his first teaching appointment in Tanzania. He returned to the University of the West Indies to teach in January of 1968.

The 1960s saw a resurgence of the mass movements in the Caribbean which had their roots in the rebellions of the 1930s. Black people everywhere began, once again, to raise the question of power, who wields it and in whose interests. In this ferment of ideas and insurrectionist mood, Walter Rodney rejected the traditional role which was ordained for the middle class in the Caribbean. Walter did not confine his activities to the cloisters and lecture rooms at the university, but shared his knowledge and exchanged ideas with the most despised and rejected elements of the Jamaican society—the Rastafari brethren.

So fertile was the ground for insurrection, that when the authorities prevented him from re-entering the country after a visit to Canada to attend a Black Writers Conference, thousands took to the streets in protest against the ban and against their own conditions of living. Several persons were killed by the police and security forces, many were injured and millions of dollars' worth of property destroyed.

Rodney's second major work was the publication of *The Groundings with My Brothers*, a collection of the talks he gave while in Jamaica.

Having been expelled from Jamaica, Walter returned to Tanzania, where he lectured from 1968 to 1974. His journey to Tanzania and other parts of Africa coincided with the armed thrust of the African liberation struggles and helped to push him even further in his belief that the intellectual should seek to deepen his/her knowledge, making it available for the struggles and emancipation of the people. It was from such a theatre that the final draft of his major work—*How Europe Underdeveloped Africa*—was sent to Bogle-L'Ouverture, in London, and was published in conjunction with Tanzanian Publishing House in 1972.

In 1974, Walter decided to return to Guyana and accepted an appointment as Professor of History at the University. The Burnham government rescinded the appointment. Once again, he soon began to give talks on African history and helped in the general awakening aimed at breaking the stranglehold which Burnham and his party held over the workers, especially at the bauxite mining town of Mackenzie. Walter threw himself into the campaign to free People's Progressive Party activist, Arnold Rampersaud, who was being held on a trumped-up charge of murder. Rodney later joined the Working People's Alliance, which was founded in 1974 and which became a political party in July, 1979.

On July 11th of that year, Walter, together with seven others, was arrested following the burning down of two government offices. He was later charged with arson. From July 1979, up to the time of his murder, the Burnham regime consistently sought him out, to persecute and harass him and, at least on one occasion, attempt to kill him. Burnham made no secret of his intentions and told Walter that he should make his will.

On the evening of June 13, 1980, agents of the government succeeded in executing what they were promising to do all along. Walter was assassinated by a bomb in the neighbourhood of his childhood haunts.

Over the years, Walter has had the support and encouragement of his wife, Pat. He was the father of three children—the eldest, Shaka, a son, and two daughters—Kanini and Asha. He also leaves behind a mother.

Thousands of people from all over the world and all walks of life will forever cherish his memory and his works.

From *Walter Rodney Memorial Programme* Kensington Town Hall, London, Friday, July 25, 1980.

INTRODUCTION

HOWARD DODSON

The emphases placed in analyzing the career of Walter Rodney have tended to accentuate one aspect at the expense of others, depending on the audience and the interpreter. Those who most appreciate his intellectual contributions play up his scholarly record of publications, while those who are more inclined to his political role emphasize his ideological contributions and his activism. Those of a Marxist persuasion place greater emphasis on his commitment to socialist theory and practice, while those of a Pan-African orientation principally embrace his strong racial identification along with his position on black power and his advocacy of African liberation.

Although the essential outlines of his life and work—his family and educational background, his academic and intellectual achievements, and his key political activities— are generally known, much less is known, and therefore said, about the complex factors that made Walter Rodney

at one and the same time a self-defined Marxist, a leading
Pan-Africanist, a revolutionary and a scholar. Moreover,
while the essential contours of Rodney's social and political
thought are manifest, the influences on its development
and the nature of its essence still remain obscure.

Walter Rodney lived with and among black and progressive peoples on four continents and in several areas of the
Caribbean. He worked in all these contexts as a historian,
university teacher, popular lecturer, social critic, and political theorist, and he was an unswerving advocate of the
oppressed and exploited classes especially those of the
black world. He was actively involved in the global struggle
for freedom. As a consequence, the actual records of his
career, his contributions, and his achievements are scattered
throughout the world. Moreover, because his life and work
embodied the synthesis of a number of seemingly contradictory dualities—Marxist vs. Pan-Africanist, activist vs.
intellectual—assessments of his political and social thought
to date have generally been partial at best, usually reflecting
a geographical specificity on one side or other of the
perceived ideological dualities. More than likely, for these
reasons, it will be some years before anything resembling a
definitive biography will be written.

In the meantime, those of us who came to know him
through working with him have the responsibility to make
what we learned available for study and careful assessment.
This responsibility is even greater when that which we
have to make available is by Walter Rodney himself. It is in
an effort to be faithful to this requirement of collective
responsibility for his legacy, and for promoting the continuing study of his life, that the Institute of the Black World
now makes available *Walter Rodney Speaks*.

In this work of sustained reflection, Walter tells us in his own words how he came to be the person that he was. He reflects on the nature and meaning of his life at a critical juncture in his career—the spring of 1975. He also discusses his views on the leading political and social trends in Africa, the Caribbean, and Black America during the mid-1970s—a period of critical shifts in Pan-African and world affairs. For all who seek to continue "grounding" with this brother, this work is essential.

Walter Rodney Speaks grew out of a program initiated by the Institute of the Black World in 1974. As noted in the preceding "Brief Biography," Walter spent the period from 1968 to 1974 in Tanzania teaching at the University of Dar es Salaam, where he completed (among other things) his most influential work, *How Europe Underdeveloped Africa* (1972). Early in 1974, however, he received an appointment as Professor of History at the University of Guyana. By the spring of that year Walter and his family had already initiated their move back to Guyana. (Indeed, by April, his wife, Pat, and their three children had already left Tanzania enroute to Guyana.)

We at the Institute of the Black World (IBW) were in touch with Walter as he planned his departure from Tanzania, and he expressed to us his interest in spending some time in the United States between leaving Dar es Salaam and returning to Guyana. At the time, we were already planning a Summer Research Symposium on the theme, "African Peoples and the International Political Economy." Knowing of Walter's keen interest in this topic and his availability, we invited him to serve as the co-director[1] and a principal faculty person for the duration of

---

[1] William Strickland, who helped plan the Symposium, served as its co-director.

the Symposium. He accepted our invitation and spent the better part of six weeks during July-September 1974 at the Institute in Atlanta. The symposium was designed to achieve the following three objectives:

1. to test the applicability of the frame of reference and the methodology used in *How Europe Underdeveloped Africa (HEUA)* for studying the evolution of political and economic relationships between black and white America;
2. to explore the structural link between the social structures of black and white America and the historical evolution of black struggle; and
3. to explore the question of the requirements of the present and future struggles of black people, especially here in the United States.

In the course of the Symposium, Walter directed his own week-long seminar. Drawing on *HEUA*, he outlined a theory and a series of methodological approaches for placing the question of black American development (and underdevelopment) in the context of the evolving U.S. and international political economies. He also presented a public lecture on the theme, "The Politics of the African Ruling Class."[2] He consulted with students in the Symposium on their respective research projects and served as a discussant during the week-long seminars conducted by

---

[2]An excerpt from the edited transcript of this lecture appeared under the same title in IBW *Black-World-Views*, Vol. I, No. 7, pp. 12-17. An audio-tape version of the complete lecture is included in the IBW cassette-tape package, "Black People and the International Crisis: Where Do We Go From Here?" Both are available through the Institute of the Black World.

most of the other Symposium faculty, Vincent Harding, Lerone Bennett Jr., Robert A. Hill, and William Strickland. Finally, he played a leading role in the conclusion to the Symposium, a seminar on "Black People and the International Crisis: Where Do We Go from Here?" Because Walter fulfilled these many roles, however, we found it impossible to carve out the necessary time to meet one other important obligation: to get him to reflect with us on his own life and work.

Walter left the United States in September 1974, in time to assume his duties as Professor of History at the University of Guyana. When the Burnham government revoked his university appointment, Walter returned to the United States to accept the invitation to teach for a semester at the Africana Studies and Research Center at Cornell University. While there, from January to May 1975, Walter finished his study on *World War II and the Tanzanian Economy* (Ithaca, N.Y.: Africana Studies and Research Monograph Series, No. 3). He also gave lectures around the country.

It was at the end of this period that Walter spent two days with Vincent Harding, Robert Hill, William Strickland and me summing up his own development and assessing the major political currents in Africa and black America. *Walter Rodney Speaks* is a product of that two-day conversation.

Shortly after the 1974 summer Symposium, IBW saw the need to reassess our mission and objectives in light of the work that had been done during the Symposium. At an IBW staff/board retreat held at Pendle Hill, Pennsylvania, we decided, among other things, to initiate a series of "roundtable" dialogues with representatives of the leading tendencies in the debate that was then raging around the issues of class vs. race, and nationalism vs. socialism. But within a week of the retreat, the offices of IBW in Atlanta were burglarized. Tapes of our discussions at Pendle Hill and other records of the meeting, in addition to a large number of IBW organizational files and office equipment, were stolen. By the end of April 1975, the offices had been burglarized two more times, and all of the IBW staff had become targets of a 24-hour-a-day campaign of harassment. Bomb threats, around-the-clock phone calls at home and at work, and threatening letters were all part of this effort, one that continued through August 1975.

While we were never able to establish the precise objectives of these attacks, we operated nonetheless on the assumption that one objective was to keep us from continuing to do our work. Having committed ourselves to carrying out the series of "roundtable" discussions, however, we decided to proceed with our plans, even in the face of these attacks. Thus, on April 30, 1975, in the midst of this organizational crisis, Harding, Hill, Strickland and I met with Rodney at the University of Massachusetts at Amherst to conduct the first IBW "roundtable" discussion.[3]

We had proposed in our initial correspondence with Walter a two-part agenda. First, following the line of development initiated in the 1974 Summer Symposium, we were interested in a further probing of the historical contradictions in black struggle and in Black America as a

---

[3]Economic and logistical considerations dictated the Amherst site. Rodney was scheduled to speak at the University of Massachusetts there on April 30, 1975. Shortly afterward he had to return to Guyana. Since Strickland was already at the University of Massachusetts at Amherst and Hill (who was teaching at Northwestern) was planning to be in the area, we decided to hold the roundtable there rather than at some other location.

whole. Second, in light of this analysis, we were interested in getting Walter's views on what he saw as an appropriate role for an organization, such as the Institute of the Black World, in helping to resolve these contradictions. Remembering the previous obligation that had gone unfulfilled, namely, a review and assessment of Walter's own intellectual and political development, we added this component to our agenda.

The discussion began around mid-day on Wednesday, April 30, and continued through the evening on Thursday, May 1, 1975—which was not only May Day but also the day that Saigon fell. Though originally conceived as a dialogue between IBW and Walter Rodney, the two days of conversation resulted in very extended expositions of Walter's viewpoints on a wide range of issues.

Robert Hill's editorial note that follows explains the principles of organization and editing used in preparing the text for publication. I should note that *Walter Rodney Speaks* is not a collection of Rodney speeches. Rather, it consists entirely of his extemporaneous responses to questions posed in the course of two days spent in dialogue with us. The text has two main sub-divisions: Part I treats his development and education in the Caribbean, England and Africa; Part II focuses on the dynamics of race and class in the black world.

The major unifying theme running through these reflections is the relationship between race and class in black political and social development, issues which had been at the center of Rodney's development. It was also a timely discussion, for the relationship between race and class had moved to the center of ideological debate within the black world by the mid-1970s. In a speech that he gave in another context during this same period, Rodney observed:

The debate which is going on is the reflection of a profound deep-seated crisis in the capitalist and imperialist
system. The fact that this debate simultaneously pro-
ceeds within the United States, within circles in Africa,
Asia and Latin America, [and] within broad communities
of students and intellectuals in Europe . . . indicates the
universalization of a particular ideological debate at this
time, and it is a reflection of the real crisis in capitalism
and imperialism. As the system fails to produce in the
real world, as the contradictions grow sharper, it
becomes incumbent upon those who are engaged in
struggle to try to find alternative means of rationalizing
the world which they perceive, because the old forms of
rationalization and projection are no longer adequate to
explaining why the crisis is what it is.[4]

This was the context in which the dialogue was held. And
while the debate has become more tempered in recent
times, it still remains perhaps the most intractable ideological issue of our time. Rodney's participation in the 1974
Symposium and the first IBW roundtable helped us to
sharpen our own analysis of this problem. *Walter Rodney
Speaks* will not only make his contribution more permanent
but through it, we are better able to see why he was the
person that could give all that he did to the struggle for
human freedom.

---

[4]Walter Rodney, untitled lecture presented at the National
Conference of Black Affairs on "Black Roots," University of
Wisconsin, Madison, April 26, 1975.

EDITOR'S STATEMENT

ROBERT A. HILL

This text was developed from transcripts of conversations held over a two-day period, April 30 and May 1, 1975, in Amherst, Massachusetts. The decision to proceed with their publication was taken only after Walter Rodney was killed, and hence we have been denied the opportunity to receive his corrections of the original transcripts as well as any changes he might have wished to make in the edited text.

The sessions were originally intended to take the form of a dialogue among Walter Rodney and the participants. For editorial reasons, however, queries and comments by the participants have been eliminated in order to achieve a smoothly flowing narrative, one that allows the reader to experience Walter Rodney without any breaks or interruptions in his reflections. The original questions and comments, and sometimes disagreements, contributed an important element to the momentum of the dialogue. They also helped significantly to deepen and clarify the responses. But having served their original purpose, it is not essential for them to be retained as part of the text at this stage.

The order in which the narrative is presented also is different to some extent from the course that the original conversations followed. The edited text concentrates on presenting the experiences and ideas that Walter Rodney recounted in their logical development. The sequence in which they emerged in the discourse criss-crossed the boundaries of place and time, sometimes in rapid succession. As much as possible, we have tried to arrange the text as a coherent and extended series of reflections, grouping the various themes within an autobiographical framework.

In a small number of instances, however, certain statements still remain somewhat ambiguous. No attempt has been made to give them any more explicit meaning than is contained in the text. Such an attempt would have been impermissible and an editorial license. However, in instances where words were inaudible but where their meaning was obvious from their context, we have simply supplied them; wherever we could not be certain, we have indicated this through the use of editorial brackets. The footnotes have been kept to a minimum. They are intended to clarify particularly important points and provide the sources of specific texts that the speaker refers to and that the reader might wish to consult.

Walter Rodney delivered many hundreds of speeches. One day, we hope, a selection of those speeches that survive will be made available. The present work will fulfill its purpose if it contributes toward that goal by providing the public with a small but significant example of Walter

Rodney's incomparable intellectual penetration, a gift that he eloquently employed in order to make the most complex political and historical subjects fully comprehensible to a popular audience.

PART I

My father was a tailor and he worked for himself as an independent artisan for most of the years of his active working life. In some very academic way you might say, therefore, he was not a member of the working class. Rather he was a member of the independent artisan class. But that would seem to be a statement that doesn't take into account all kinds of realities of the Caribbean situation. The very term "working class" of course, in my opinion, has to be liberally or creatively interpreted in our own situation. We have very few workers directly in production in the kind of way that is implied by the Marxian model.

My father from time to time did move into a more regular wage-labor situation. He did, for instance, work sometimes for a big tailoring establishment, where he went in and he was simply assigned jobs and was paid a wage each week. But, generally speaking, that was considered as a desperate measure—when one could not make it on one's own, one would accept work in the big tailoring establishment, because while the wage was steady, it was always smaller.

My mother was also a housewife and a part-time seamstress. And my grandparents on both sides were farmers essentially. And again I can't really say that they were peasantry. They belong to some different class. In my mind they are the working class, for they are the producers of wealth, the people who work with their labor, alienated in the Guyanese context.

I grew up in a divided society, in which the majority of one's day-to-day contacts were with one's own ethnic group. There was a certain isolation, but I did not regard it as a condition of hostility. One interrelated with Indian families and with Indians at school. They were just other Guyanese. But there was that sense that they were out there and that there was the potential rivalry and that one had to be on guard. The images that were common in the black community were images, for instance, which set one to thinking that one must of necessity maintain certain standards because the alternative would be the threat of being overcome by Indians. It was a curious kind of double-standard. In one way it was anti-Indian; in another sense it raised the Indians to a position of the ideal almost. Black people had a way of saying: "you see those Indian students. They go to school and they go back home and they help their parents. So you must help your parents. You see that Indian fellow there, he isn't spending his time round some jukebox joint. He's studying hard. So one must study". It was in a sense competitive and contradictory, but it was almost an idealization. I don't think it is really true, in fact, about Indian dedication, solidarity, and that sort of thing. Black people were always saying, we're so divided, the

Indians all move together; or, on the cultural level, Indians still have their names, still have their clothes. We don't have anything.

At the same time, we had to try and come to terms with the fundamental illusion that education would resolve everything. Indeed, for a few people it resolves most things in their own personal or private lives. The consequence is that both the African and Indian people of Guyana have created this tradition of sending their children to school at great sacrifice and ensuring that one or more of their children move out of their working-class or producer-class background by virtue of education. The framework of the society is accepted and upward mobility within that framework is all that matters.

But more than that, one of its unfortunate consequences is that it produces this fantastic exodus of the West Indian intellectual. It is very obvious that within the expectations and within this model of achievement, the society in fact doesn't have room for so many people at the top. It's only an illusion that by education you will move up into the class at the top and earn a certain salary and live a certain way. And when people reach close to the top they find that (a) there is no room within the society, and (b) there is a greater saleability [elsewhere] of those skills which they have learned because, having become a commodity, they can rise up in the commodity market which is wider than Guyana. It includes Canada, the United States, etc. Therefore the best of our people have traditionally just reached a certain point and just moved out through the conduits that lead out of our society. They have moved out into the wider capitalist world. Again, for some, very often their parents and their families are quite pleased about this. They are quite pleased to say, we have such and such a son who is a doctor in Ontario, Canada. But, needless to say, he isn't curing any disease in Guyana.

Yet, there is something positive about the approach (and I found the same approach in Africa), which is a commitment to be serious and to take education very seriously. I have taught in Africa and I have taught in the Caribbean, and I have met a large number of black students in this country [i.e., in the U.S.] and from this country. There just isn't that same degree of commitment. In my opinion, the African student is highest in his or her motivation, and then comes the Caribbean student, and then the black American. This is going to pose problems in the future in the United States, because in the new society that we expect to build, we will need to understand that we must develop our own commitment to study, to scholarship, to art, to whatever we're doing, to take it extremely seriously.

Ironically, the black person in this society in many ways is the most advanced at a given level of perception. They have perceived that the system is essentially fraudulent. This is what brothers and sisters here see, which many Africans and West Indians have not yet perceived. It is because we [West Indians and Africans] take the system seriously, at its own evaluation, that we want to move up within it, and so there is that dedication to get there. However, brothers and sisters here in America perceive the sham of the system. They say, we're not into that at all. That's foolishness. That's the white man's game. What really matters is to "make it" somehow. So better to hustle and "make it" than to fall into the trap of thinking that producing term papers really will make you a scholar.

This attitude has a strength, but its weakness is that it fails to confront an old decaying order with a new discipline, with a new mental and intellectual discipline, with new habits of work, etc. It tends to escape in ways that really are characteristic of the system, because to say that one will hustle and "make it" is really to fall into the trap which the system sets. Yes, we must have our work ethic and it's a very important ongoing factor, provided we don't take ourselves too seriously, or take the system seriously, provided we move towards understanding that we're working seriously to establish an alternative, as distinct from working seriously to participate in the system.

The reason why the Africans are at the top of the pole in this regard is because, even though there is a lot more appearance than reality, there is still the definite appearance that they have the opportunity to recreate their society after their own image. After all, you teach an African student in a university this year, and next year he's in the Ministry of Finance as a permanent secretary. He's actually making policy, trying to construct, in his own way, the lives of his people and intervening in history in a manner in which the black student in [the U.S.] knows he will never, in this sytem, be able to do. I think the immediacy of the possibility of participating in change is a critical variable.

EARLY EXPERIENCES

My own limited experience incorporated two principal elements and a third element which is secondary or tertiary if you like. The first, and the most important one, was growing up in Guyana at a time when, as a primary school student, the People's Progressive Party (PPP) was organizing and mobilizing on the nationalist question. The PPP was the first mass party in Guyana and it was also a multi-racial party. It was at that time the only party in the West

Indies which had any pretensions about having a scientific socialist outlook or Marxist outlook or working-class outlook. It came ultimately into conflict with the British and the Americans on this score, so that whatever little constitutional gains were made in 1953, were removed when the British suspended the constitution.

But that period was very significant in my life, because what it did for me was to raise in my own mind a conviction about the seriousness and potentiality of our own people. My parents, particularly my father, were involved in the early formation of the PPP. I knew those individuals who would come to our house or to whose house my father would go to discuss political organization. As a youngster, I was given the sort of humdrum task to distribute party manifestos which one doesn't necessarily understand, but you come up against certain things. How does a person react when you say to them, here is a PPP manifesto? Do they take it with sympathy? Do they buy a rosette or one of the things that you're trying to sell for the party? Do they chase you away? Do they take it contemptuously? Do they, as happened in one instance, set their dog on you so that you run out of their house? After a while, without knowing anything about class, I knew that there were certain kinds of Guyanese into whose yard one did not go to carry a PPP manifesto. You could tell from the kind of house or the shade or complexion of the lady reclining, sipping her tea, or whatever she may be doing. You don't intervene in that situation and say, "Read a PPP manifesto, we're asking for workers to do this and that."

This was at age eleven. You just have to have a sense of survival, rather than class consciousness, because they might have an Alsatian dog under the house, and they let it loose on you. This was my first real introduction to the class question. One avoided those places and one began to understand that the houses where there were no long driveways as where you could just go right up and knock and certain people would come out and they'd welcome you. Some people would even tell you they don't want the manifesto because we're already voting PPP. They would tell you this in Guyanese speech pattern. And others would say, you don't need to come and convince us, you don't need to spend any time distributing this. We understand. We are for this. These were very ordinary people.

This was at a time when the church was against the PPP and sermons used to be preached against the PPP. Roman Catholic churches were known for that. And yet, amazingly, the people came out and they voted for the PPP, although they had been told all kinds of things—that they would go to hell and that there would be damnation and suffering and so on if we have communism. But, without fully understanding anything that was going on, the struggle just made sense to me. Often, there was a certain pride you could feel among people, because people were making a choice of their own. They weren't being swayed by the traditional people who ordered us around.

When you went out to political meetings you also saw people that you knew. My mother, who was a simple woman, would walk far distances from our house to go to political meetings, perhaps carrying a little bench in her hand so that ultimately she could sit down, since these meetings lasted for hours. One expected to hear at least a dozen major speakers who would come on and give rousing speeches. Each one of them had names that they carried like "the Bengal Tiger," etc. These were our people expressing themselves in a way that they certainly weren't taught in secondary school. Because I knew from my little experience, and I moved on into secondary school shortly after, that the schools were very hostile to this kind of manifestation. Secondary schools weren't about training people to express themselves for the people. There was training in what was called debating, which was to talk about nothing provided you said nothing as cleverly as possible and as entertainingly as possible. Then you got full marks. If you said anything too substantial, your marks would come down.

So I feel that I had a grasp and a confidence that our people have the capacity to deal with their own situation, and that has not changed in me since. With all the vicissitudes of racial struggle that went on in Guyana, I have seen what my parents did and I have seen what other people's parents did, and what people we call 'neighbor' and 'cousin' also did. They were not political ideologues, but ordinary people taking their destiny into their own hands.

THE INITIAL IMPULSE TOWARD SOCIALISM

As a young primary schoolboy up until 1953, and then as a secondary school student after that, there was a whole generation of already adult young Guyanese—the Martin Carters and so on—who were participating in the political events of 1953, and who were extremely creative and extremely revolutionary at the same time. I myself would like to do a little bit more to find out exactly what was the process of formation of that generation of our intellectuals and exactly what the year 1953 did to them. I mention Martin Carter because he is one of the very few who is still around, while many other people have scattered. I can see what the society has done to him.

As distinct from the many writers, poets and artists, who I think ultimately were the more important figures, there was later a small segment that went into the university and came up in an academic environment, like C.Y. Thomas and myself. We took with us, sometimes unknowingly, a willingness to accept at least the concepts of socialism/communism/Marxism/class struggle without any *a priori* rejection which many of our university colleagues did have. Many of the people with whom I was training at the University of the West Indies, Jamaicans in particular, were technically as skilled as any of us, but they had this fundamental reservation about socialist and Marxist thought which I don't think Clive Thomas and I ever shared. That was because the PPP was the only mass party in Guyana and the leadership explicitly said, "we are socialists, we are Marxists". And they were prepared to talk about creating a new anti-capitalist society based on a new and different theory or perception than the one to which which we were accustomed. So that long before many Guyanese entered into a serious examination of what was Marxism and communism, at least it seemed to us, from what we heard the leadership of the PPP and the party saying, that whatever Marxism, socialism, and these various concepts meant, they were things that could be taken seriously.

These were things that one did not put beyond the pale, because of a series of conditioning factors which told you that they were taboo, and therefore the limits of your thoughts must always stop before you arrive there. I have never had that barrier. That's probably why my own development has been sort of very incremental. It didn't have to take a flying leap at some point over the unknown. I didn't have to break with some very serious religious or moral or philosophical concepts or any fears that might have even had roots in my psyche—fears that somehow I was going to take up something that was evil. For many other Third World scholars coming up in a rather different context, they have had to make this breakthrough. They have been forced to make almost a moral choice about socialism. They have had to say, how are we going to grapple with that evil thing? Of course, later on they find out that it isn't evil, but the bogey-man is there in their minds. I don't think it has been there in the minds of my immediate generation of Guyanese colleagues.

I don't want the impression to be left that there was mass political education in Guyana. I'm speaking here of a certain receptivity, a certain set of attitudes as well as a substantive acquaintance with Marxism. One of the problems in Guyana was that we did not, in fact, get that mass political education for a variety of reasons. The British intervened. I also think that the PPP did not understand the necessity to really sink roots as a party of political education because they were concerned with electoral politics. What I'm speaking of here is simply a receptivity to the idea of socialism.

THE DYNAMISM OF THE JAMAICAN PEOPLE

The second element that was important to my development was my experience of the Jamaican people, who are a breed apart, in my estimation, of any people. Students from the eastern Caribbean who went to university in Jamaica were struck by the dynamism of the people in Jamaica. There is a different pace of life in Jamaica, probably due to the fact that the population is larger and more concentrated. But there definitely is a greater pace. Trinidadians try to assume the role of city slickers almost, and are clever and fast, but for staying power, for sheer energy, Jamaican

people seem to have us all beat. It's not surprising that
there should be a universalizing tendency when different
Caribbean people get together to fall into certain Jamaican
idioms, certainly to use the swear words. Jamaicans can
curse more proficiently than any other Caribbean people.
They have such a range of words describing phenomena so
neatly and I think this is a testimony to their combativeness.
So that I always felt that there must be tremendous
revolutionary potential in that island.

One also saw it when one went to London. The Jamaicans
were the largest group in London and they were also the
most important group. I would really say that their sense of
combativeness nipped British racism in the bud. Jamaicans
had a way of striking back that did not brook too much
playing about. I think that, if in those formative years, the
small black population in Britain had quietly submitted to
some of the things that a few Englishmen were putting on
them, then such practices would have become more generalized and white people would have walked all over black
people at any time. But Jamaicans would behave in what I
used to think was an amazingly bellicose and provocative
manner, given the conditions of disadvantage in strength.
We blacks were few and the whites were many. But
Jamaicans would take on a whole railway station if
necessary, and would move forward to single out a white
man, snatch him and hit him. The lesson was learnt. After a
while, when you met people in England and you said you
were from the West Indies, they would say, "Oh, you're a
Jamaican."

Some Guyanese and Trinidadians got a little upset at this
because they were also supposed to be a little more rowdy
and those of us who thought we were more *urbane* didn't
want to be called a Jamaican. It was a put-down. But for

others, we recognized that it was also a form of protection because the Jamaican brothers were out there in the street defending the whole race, as it were. And I knew for sure that a people, not just Jamaicans, but all of us West Indians, who could defend themselves in that way and who could come straight from a rural environment (sell their land in St. Kitts or in some little island in the Grenadines, and come to London and start over), run the underground system, run the buses, run the hospitals, take over the schools—people who could do that clearly were people who had almost unlimited capacity for change. This wasn't being taught inside the context of the Caribbean.

THE MASS MOVEMENT IN TRINIDAD

In addition to these two types of experiences, the Guyanese and Jamaican, with the Jamaican coming much later, there was a third but lesser experience. Trinidians did very well for themselves in the 1950s because they had a tremendous mass movement, though it has long since been dissipated.

Looking at these three experiences, I felt that whatever may be the political direction in the Caribbean at a given point in time, one must always identify the level of the mass movement and differentiate it from the kinds of politics that are actually being carried out by the local ruling class. We should differentiate between seeing a viable political movement in operation and having confidence in the capacity of the people to create a movement. I have real confidence in the people's capacity in the West Indies to create change.

THE NATIONALIST PILGRIMAGE

I have tried to put myself back in time and ask myself

where my head was at in, say, 1960 or 1963. There are a host of perceptions which at that time I would not have recognized as being very important, but which with hindsight mattered.

On the whole, being in the field of history helped. I was at the University of the West Indies at a time when at least the university had begun the nationalist pilgrimage. University faculty and students in disciplines such as history and in other fields such as economics, politics, and sociology had made the breakthrough against a purely externally oriented kind of syllabus. I call this essentially the nationalist phenomenon, where we have defined ourselves as a people, as a nation, and have then asked: now how do we overturn this old absurd history?

One of my earliest pieces of writing goes back to those early years [Walter Rodney and C. Augustus, "The Negro Slave," *Caribbean Quarterly* 10(1964): 40-47]. It was written as an undergraduate, and was about the way that slaves were treated and perceived.

This was very meaningful to me at that time, and looking back at it now I have no real disagreement with the position. It's just that I wouldn't feel it necessary to state such a position now and I should hope that most people don't need to restate such basics. But then it was necessary that one come to grips with the way in which one's being, and the presentation of one's being, was so hopelessly distorted by the sources to which one went for scholarship.

The faculty and program at UWI were helpful in this regard. They were at least raising the nationalist question and by raising the nationalist question it ultimately pointed me, for instance, in the direction of Africa. From Caribbean history, from looking at the slave trade, one decided that one needed to understand slavery and understand the cultural background of Africa.

There was a certain professor at the university, with whom I subsequently came to have a lot of differences, but who had an essay assignment which he gave to each group of incoming students as the very first thing to do before anything else. It was an essay which asked students to look at Europe and Africa and their relevance to the Caribbean. I attempted to answer that by suggesting that both Europe and Africa were equally important. But, as I recall it, I could readily illustrate why I thought that Europe was important. I had a facility for drawing upon a range of common historical assumptions which I shared with the British at that time, and still do actually, to indicate why Europe was relevant. But I could only say Africa was relevant at a sort of intuitive level. Outside of some vague generalizations, I couldn't articulate why Africa was relevant. So eventually it was necessary to move in that direction.

THE SIGNIFICANCE OF ERIC WILLIAMS AND C. L. R. JAMES

When we were studying at the university in Jamaica, C. L. R. James' *Black Jacobins* [New York: Vantage Books, 1963] and Eric Williams' *Capitalism and Slavery* [New York: Capricorn Books, 1966] were really two of the foremost texts that informed a nationalist consciousness. At that time it wasn't very clear that the methodology and the ideology of these two works were significantly different from anything else that we were reading. What was clear was that here were people taking a perspective that appealed to us as young West Indians. One must say this clearly in the case of *Capitalism and Slavery*, since we don't want to get confused by the fact that its author became involved in other things. We want to understand that the work is historically important, that Williams was making points about what slavery and capitalism were about, and that these were both intellectually and emotionally appealing. One could recognize one's self in that history. One could feel with it. And this was certainly even more the case with *The Black Jacobins*, which was about black people involved in revolution, involved in making choices, involved in real movements of history, in which there were splits and some people fell by the wayside, but which also possessed a tremendous underlying strength and represented a real achievement.

Later on, of course, I got to understand, especially as I started to sift through the historiography of the Haitian Revolution, how it was that certain conceptual tools, ideological tools—a Marxist methodology, had informed James' work and was responsible in large part for raising its quality over and above that of several other attempted formulations on the revolution. James exercised a sort of model image for many young West Indian progressives. Again, and even before one had fully come to terms with the question of Marxist ideology, he did stand out in the Trinidadian situation as the person who seemed to be making more sense than others.[1] It was as simple as that.

------

[1]C.L.R. James returned to Trinidad in April 1958, and, at the request of the People's National Movement (PNM), he edited the party's weekly newspaper, *The Nation*, for two years. He was also secretary of the West Indian Federal Labour Party during the same period. He resigned both posts in 1960. For an account of James' political differences with the leadership of Dr. Eric Williams, see C.L.R. James, *Party Politics in the West Indies* (Port of Spain, Trinidad: Vedic Enterprises, 1962); see also Ivar Oxaal, *Black Intellectuals Come to Power: The Rise of Creole Nationalism in Trinidad and Tobago* (Cambridge, Mass.: Schenkman Publishing Co., 1968); and Selwyn D. Ryan, *Race and Nationalism in Trinidad and Tobago: A Study of Decolonization in the Multiracial Society* (Toronto: University of Toronto Press, 1972).

He seemed to be willing to go further. He seemed to be most complete in his acceptance of the necessity for the Trinidadian (and ultimately the West Indian) people to make a break with their past.

And, of course, C.L.R. James was known in Guyana. He was known to me then just as a figure. One didn't know who he was, but one noticed the effect that C.L.R. James had when he came into town. And many people would go to hear him because it would be a curiosity to go and hear somebody who is called a Marxist and was a well-known black figure. You may also have heard the word Trotskyite bandied about somewhere. So you really had to turn up to see who this creature was, this black man who is a Marxist and a Trotskyite, and who apparently is saying some important things to which people have to listen.

But later on, at the university in Jamaica, C.L.R. James did exercise this force as a kind of a model figure. And more recently, in my own life and thought, he's remained a model in a specific kind of way, not in the sense that I feel any commitment to pursue positions which he has adopted *per se*. But, as he has grown older—and as I have looked around me and recognized how the struggle creates so many casualties (and somehow along the line physiology plays a part) and how the older people get the more they seem to opt out of any revolutionary struggle, seem to wane, seem to take up curious positions that are actually reversals of where they earlier stood—James has become a model of the possibilities of retaining one's intellectual and ideological integrity over a protracted period of time. In other words, I've always said to myself that I hoped that at his age, if I'm around, I still have some credibility as a progressive, that people wouldn't look around and say, "This used to be a revolutionary."

TRAVEL TO THE SOVIET UNION AND CUBA

Yet I don't think really in that period of 1960-63, I had any serious awareness of the need not simply to study black history and Africa, but to go beyond that and to see it from a different ideological perspective. There were, however, a number of experiences that were useful. One was travelling and visiting places.

When I travelled to the Soviet Union, I was struck on arrival at the airport by the physical demeanor and the social aspect of the people in the airport. They were workers and peasants, as far as I could see, who were flying on those TU-104's to Moscow, to Leningrad, etc., as though they were using a bus. And my understanding of an airport was that it was a very bourgeois institution. There were only certain of us who were supposed to be in an airport. But the Soviets seemed to have ascended beyond that. That was what one confronted going into the country. And then, having left the airport, one goes out into the streets and one is amazed at the number of books they sell—in the streets, on the pavement, all over. In my society, you have to search for a bookstore and be directed and told that *the* bookstore is down *that* street, as if it's an alien institution. And even in America, one can buy hot dogs and hamburgers on the sidewalks, a lot of nice things like that, but not books.

And it seemed to me that there was something different about this Soviet society. There was also something different about seeing ordinary people going into the Bolshoi Ballet, because I had previously been to London and I passed by the West End and I had seen the London upper classes going to their opening-night performances. Again the difference was striking. Those things remained with me and they still do.

Travelling to Cuba was also another important experience, because I was with Cuban students and I got some insight at an early period into the tremendous excitement of the Cuban Revolution. This was 1960, just after the victory of the revolution. One has to live with a revolution to get its full impact, but the next best thing is to go there and see a people actually attempting to grapple with real problems of development.

Cuba was a different dimension from the Soviet Union, because the Russians had made their revolution and were moving along smoothly. But the Cubans were up and about, talking and bustling and running and jumping and really living the revolution in a way that was completely outside of anything that one could read anywhere or listen to or conceptualize in an island such as Jamaica, which is where I was still. The Cuban experience was very good. I was fortunate in visiting Cuba twice, only for brief periods, but long enough to get that fire and dynamic of the Cuban revolution.

It has bothered me for a decade and a half, and remains a constant bugbear still, that the West Indian intellectual class was so lazy that it never seriously attempted to come to grips with the Cuban experience. It seemed to me that whatever was going on there, it clearly was important enough to warrant analysis, if nothing else. And yet, here we were in our intellectual debasement! One result was that whenever we might marginally touch upon socialism, in discussion, it was as an abstraction. For we could never relate it to the fact that some people were actually about building a socialist society ninety miles away.

I don't say that it was this that made me a Marxist, but it was one of the little levers which, in looking back on it, probably did help my moving in a different ideological direction.

LENIN AS A REVOLUTIONARY INTELLECTUAL

Finally, there were confrontations in the university classroom with the same tutors who were essentially nationalist progressives, but who, as I found subsequently, hadn't made the break with class.

There was one individual who was very anti-Cuban, and that bothered me. There was another individual who made a statement which has constantly remained with me. I was doing some paper on the Russian Revolution and it struck me that this Lenin was a person who had a tremendous capacity for intellectualizing and at the same time doing. In my own naïve way, I called this phenomenon "a revolutionary intellectual." But the professor was very hard on this statement. He said: "There is no such thing. One can be an intellectual or one can be revolutionary. You can't combine the two. Lenin may at one time have been a revolutionary, at another time an intellectual, but the moment he moves into practical activity he must abandon intellectualism."

This was a most curious argument. Even at that time I thought it was most curious, but with my own naïveté I couldn't really confront the argument. I just sensed that something was wrong about it. And I felt that somehow being a revolutionary intellectual might be a goal to which one might aspire, for surely there was no real reason why one should remain in the academic world—that is, remain an intellectual—and at the same time not be revolutionary. So I bore that in mind, and the fact that I do recall it very clearly does indicate that.

IN ENGLAND

These were the beginnings of my journey toward "Marxism" or socialism, and after that things speeded up. In

Britain, I became more and more conscious, more directed towards an objective.

First of all, here I was within the society which had dominated our way of thinking in the British Caribbean. It's the kind of experience which has to be lived to be understood, for it's very difficult to communicate to others. Probably the only people who have succeeded in some measure in communicating what it means to be a colonial going to the metropole have been the novelists, because there is an emotive quality that must be conveyed by the artist. There are a host of emotions and fears, phobias and illusions and disillusionments that come from looking at that very, very cold society: the cold buildings, the cold people, the cold food, and everything else that one has to come up against.

Here was I, as a young migrant if you like, part of a migrant community, but functioning in exactly the same way as most of my brothers and sisters who were worker-migrants. They were directly involved in production. They had to deal with discrimination where it mattered, at the job and in getting a job; and having got the job, they had to deal with discrimination in housing, which as a student, if you wanted to, you could avoid. In fact, though, I was living outside the university all the time, so that I did have a touch of what it meant to go to doors in answer to an advertisement and knock and be told that it was already taken once the landlady perceived the color of my face.

My experience of English society, of its racism, and of its exploitation was in a sense second-hand. Yet I understood it, because I lived among West Indian workers and I understood what it meant to be part of the most exploited section of the working class in that society. Even though I was in school, my brother was at work and my roommate was at work. My wife worked later on when we got married.

The person with whom I lived was a Guyanese woman whom we all called "Mums." She was a surrogate mother for a lot of young people and she was a worker in the broad sense of the word: part-time housekeeper, part-time day-carer for children, and part-time seamstress working as an extension of London's sweating trade at a very low rate. So I was part of that working community. Very quickly, but largely through my brother, who already had had very rich experiences in being a member of the British Air Force (he had served in Cyprus) and who was already involved in political life, I moved immediately into trying to learn from the mass of migrant workers.

I used to be involved on a regular platform at Hyde Park throughout the period I was in London. In those years a lot of West Indians turned up at Hyde Park. It was, of course, a place where a number of freak shows were also held, a place where things were said that weren't serious. But quite a number of West Indians did go there as a meeting place, as an expression of the fact that they were under pressure and they wanted to find ways of talking and dealing with their exploitation and with racism. Thus I was involved there for three years, every summer. From the time it got warm enough to speak until the time when it was too cold to speak, I would be on the platform at Hyde Park.

In this period of my life and with the necessity to relate to working people, I was consciously beginning to read Marxism more extensively. At the end of my stay at the University of the West Indies, Marx came in as one component in a "Political Thought" course. But now for the first time, I realized that this was not just material within a course, or a segment within the totality of bourgeois knowledge, but that it had something fundamentally different to offer. Also one began to look more closely at the Marxist experience *per se*, at transformational experiences such as China, which had an important emotional appeal because it was a non-white country at a time when one's racial consciousness was very high.

AMONG THE ACADEMIC ESTABLISHMENT

Finally, to complete this picture of my evolution, I of course had to battle things out in my academic work. I was a research student and I had set myself a certain task, which was to complete a Ph.D. program. It was a typical objective to which the West Indian student who comes to London would aspire. It was not in any way different from the normal movement away from a working-class background and towards a petit-bourgeois social formation.

I recall that when I first went up to the School of Oriental and African Studies (SOAS), the question was raised as to whether or not I had to take some qualifying exams or do some papers in their undergraduate work. Now, I had always understood that somebody who got first-class honors at a university was entitled to continue to do postgraduate research. And I had this naïve impression that since the University College of the West Indies, (which it was when I started my degree) was one of the constituent colleges of the University of London, then there could be no question—that it was just as though I had come from down the road at King's College or somewhere else. But this was not so.

I had come from the colonies. You may call UCWI a college of the University of London, but their missionaries had set that up and it doesn't necessarily mean that it has the same standards as that which they claim to possess. This was the attitude of some people. In other words, the issue had to be debated. Ultimately, it was said, "Oh well, the University College of the West Indies, the first-class honors, we can accept this". It wasn't as automatic as if I had come from the University of Durham, outside of the London system, with first-class honors. I know that those students, in fact, some of them with second-class honors, would have immediately gone on to do their research.

So one had to vindicate oneself. The colonial had to show that colonized people had the same capacity. And this was a typical response to the colonial student. The moment you go there you're under that load, that you're not just you, but you are a representative of a whole people, who have been victimized, and who not only have been victimized but who are also regarded as the agents of their own victimization and that something is somehow wrong with them.

The outcome was that I was forced to try and formulate something that was intellectually different and yet in a sense acceptable to the academic establishment. And I really was among the establishment. SOAS had at that time the two most important British scholars on Africa, Roland Oliver and John D. Fage. Fage then left to found the Centre [of West African Studies] at [the University of] Birmingham, but he came back for seminars.

SOAS was set up in Britain to train colonial administrators to go out to administer the empire. But then after World War II the empire unaccountably collapsed. Africans had taken this unconscionable step, unforgiveable step. Those who ruled the empire then had to find, firstly, Europeans who would continue to play a role in the neo-colonial setting, and, more importantly, to find bright young men—not in the sense C.L.R. James writes of Kwame Nkrumah[2]—who would serve the purposes of Europeans, who would become part of the world of

[2]C.L.R. James, *Nkrumah and the Ghana Revolution* (London: Allison and Busby, 1977).

European scholarship, and who would represent, in effect, extensions to the highest levels in universities back in the Third World.

I perceived SOAS then, and I perceive it even more clearly now—at the least the African section—as very involved in the defense of bourgeois ideology. We had weekly seminars every Tuesday afternoon, the most urbane seminar that you could think of, led by all these deans of knowledge on Africa, who had this tremendous flair for keeping everybody at a lower level. Even if one were an African or a West Indian, and one wanted to talk about the questions [raised] in the seminar, they could dominate partly because of their greater expertise, and familiarity with the paper, and partly because, after all, they had been at this for a long time. They represented the outgrowth of centuries of an intellectual tradition, and this is just not to be scoffed at.

One way of dealing with it, of course, is simply to abandon the seminars and say, some things are going on in that room with which I can't deal, with which I don't want to deal. But for various reasons, my own response was to try and cope with it. I was fortunate really, for I had a very sympathetic supervisor [Richard Gray]. In the British system that matters because you have a single individual supervisor and not a committee. And if he really wants to do you in, he can. If he is very sympathetic, he can also help to put you over a lot of hurdles. And my supervisor was a liberal bourgeois historian who had, to my mind, certain basic skills as well as integrity. And he made a lot of effort, I would say, even went out of his way, to accommodate my own development and my own view. Perhaps if this was not so, I might have been forced to take another stand. But I thought he was very helpful.

Therefore, I felt that I should stick to the task of achieving this academic degree, of coming up to the standards that they set in terms of the collection of data and its presentation. One had to master that because, if one didn't, it was as though one was speaking out of "sour grapes." One could never challenge them unless one was up to those criteria. In a way it was a good thing, too, because even if some of the extensive reading was reading of useless material which, in the end, you found out was loaded and ideologically very hostile, nevertheless, it was an intellectual exercise, a mental exercise that lent discipline. When one went into a seminar, there were people there who always knew a great deal of details and you had to master as much as possible so that your thesis wouldn't be shot full of holes merely on some pedantic considerations. And, ultimately, I thought that was useful.

There is a certain distance which one has to go in trying to meet the so-called standards. But beyond that it becomes self-defeating and ridiculous. And the question is, where is the cut-off point? To claim that the standards are irrelevant is never really to attack the world of bourgeois scholarship. Rather, it is simply to leave it in the hands of the enemy, as it were.

But to see those standards as encompassing one's existence for all times is even more self-defeating, because you simply become another bourgeois academic. The format in which you operate, the journals in which you publish, the language in which you express yourself, the people to whom you feel responsible for justifying this or that position, the books that you are called upon to review and so on, makes you a part of this bourgeois academic community.

For example, in terms of scholarly apparatus, it is not

just the fact of footnoting, but whom you footnote. The game is to show that, after all, if one is in a given field, you must start with so and so and come down the line and pay your deference to each one of these authorities through your intellectual work. That is ultimately self-defeating, and in fact has quite clearly defeated a number of us who have entered this field. Indeed, I would say it has defeated more than have actually managed to transcend it.

One of my objectives in writing *How Europe Underdeveloped Africa* [London: Bogle-L'Ouverture Publishers, 1972] was to defeat this, to attack it, and to circumvent it. It was to insure that I didn't remain a victim of presenting material in a context and in a form where it was only accessible to certain kinds of people. And among several other things, this text was designed to operate outside of the university. It might get into the university, yes. I hoped it would. But it was designed to operate from outside in the sense that it would not be sponsored by the people who considered themselves, and whom many others considered, to be the ones at that time who had the last word to say on African history and African studies. The aim of this publication was to reach our own people without having it mediated by the bourgeois institutions of learning.

The ideology of all this I had to work out for myself. For there was nobody in that SOAS seminar, during the whole of the three years I was there, who could remotely be termed a Marxist, a quasi-Marxist, or a neo-Marxist of any variety of gender whatsoever. People talk about the London School of Economics as a place where there were some progressive and even Marxist elements from time to time. But SOAS was not a school in that sense.

It was thus a painful process of trying to read Marxism on one's own and applying it to the historical data. I think some of that comes out in *The History of the Upper Guinea*

Coast, 1545 to 1800 [Oxford: The Clarendon Press, 1970].
Looking at that work now, I would certainly not see it as a
strong statement of Marxian scholarship by any means. It
was just strong enough, let's say, to upset some members of
the establishment who perceived the direction in which I
was trying to move. As far as those at SOAS were
concerned, so long as it met their own criteria for being a
work of scholarship, it didn't do any harm. And, perhaps, it
even did some good. Because it showed, well, we have a
young black protégé here. We can allow him to say some of
these things that are a little off-colour, but he is one of us.
Ultimately, he will understand the reality of things, become
an African professor, come to our scholarly conferences
and participate in the general evolution of our point of view.

It is interesting that my early work, which I considered to
be at a low level in Marxian terms, received much more
hostile responses in the United States than it did in Britain.
This is an interesting commentary on the level of American
sensitivity to Marxian scholarship. The United States is
much more backward in that respect. The Europeans, and
even the British with their hostility to Marxism, have a
sophistication with which they deal with these matters. It
was very clear from some of the reviews that certain
American scholars just felt hurt or wounded that anybody
should dare to even begin to suggest that there was
something like a class analysis, or that when we are dealing
with slavery in Africa, we must put it in the context of
capitalism and not just see two abstract sets of bodies
[Europe and Africa] meeting with each other.[3]

---

[3]Philip D. Curtin, *Journal of African History* 11 (1970): 453-55;
D.F. McCall, *American Historical Review* 76 (June 1971): 813;
M.A. Klein, *Social Studies* 62 (November 1971): 251-252.

STUDY GROUP WITH C.L.R. JAMES

So that was the period, up until 1966, when I was grappling on my own with these ideas in the academic institution in which I found myself. I was, of course, relating to the odd Marxists outside. But, generally speaking, the political climate in Britain, especially on the Left, was not conducive to the development of any independent Marxist thought.

There was nothing on the English political scene as such that was helpful. On the other hand, there was a study group experience which several of us had with C.L.R. James and his wife Selma James. Getting together in London and meeting over a period of two to three years on a fairly regular basis afforded me the opportunity that I, and a number of other people were seeking—to acquire a knowledge of Marxism, a more precise understanding of the Russian Revolution, and of historical formulation.

One of the most important things which I got out of that experience was a certain sense of historical analysis, in the sense that C.L.R. James was really a master of the analysis of historical situations. It was not enough to study Lenin's *State and Revolution*. It was important to understand why it was written and what was going on in Russia at that precise point in time. It was not enough to study Lenin's *What Is to Be Done*. One must understand the specific contextual nature of the discussions that were going on in Russia at that time. This comes to my mind because I feel that a lot of the debates that do go on about Marxism are definitely out of context. People pull from texts without knowing the history of those texts and the [context] of the debates in which they were located. One thing is certain about C.L.R. James—he has mastered a whole range of theory and historical data and analysis. This explains why he was very good at focusing in. The group might do some reading and try to understand what a text says. But James gave it that added dimension which nobody else in the group could easily acquire in being able to say: this is what Lenin was about; this is what Trotsky was doing; he had just come from this conference or this debate, or this was his specific programmatic objective when he was writing, and so on.

That was a very important experience which I am still pondering. I see its significance more as one goes along and I recognize the necessity for us to do much more work of that type.

Of course, as many people know, C.L.R. had that habit of really incisively dismissing bourgeois foolishness. And I think that his wife, Selma James, in her own right had a complementary if different style that tended in that same direction.

I should say something about Selma James, C.L.R. James' wife. What a very unusual woman! She sometimes, even more than C.L.R., had this habit of taking a foolish position and really indicating why that position was foolish. When Selma was finished indicating why it was foolish, one had very little doubt about its foolishness. She did, along with C.L.R., exemplify the power of Marxist thought. That's what one got—a sense that a bourgeois argument could never really stand a chance against a Marxist argument, provided one was clear about it. After a while it became self-evident. It became ludicrous to attempt to put forward a bourgeois position. And it was helpful to us to understand that you didn't go into some discussion with them and bring there some high-sounding ideas that you had read by one of the leading bourgeois critics, or even a serious Marxist. You couldn't do that and get away with it in the presence of C.L.R. and Selma James.

THE BRITISH LEFT

There was no possibility for Marxist development within the old Left. There were still the old Communist party types and the old Trotskyite types. There were also one or two young Trotskyites from the colonies. Together they called themselves the Trotskyite movement. From then and until now, I've always found it difficult to understand what Trotskyism is because I couldn't really get anything out of these people's positions. It tended to be inarticulate. It tended to be whimsical. It tended to be downright foolish on many questions. And this was not my understanding of Trotsky's role in the Russian Revolution. But, nevertheless, I didn't press that issue.

All I knew was that I didn't want to be in some of these movements that were called Marxist—neither the Communist party, which was old and effete with an average age, it seemed to me, of about 60 or 65, with most everybody there past working age, nor the Trotskyites, who were something else again, the result of a period of sectarianism that had gone on for decades. One would come across Trotskyite factions within which I found majority and minority elements. And then I heard about factions! And one would go to conferences and you would find that there was a faction comprising two people. They had been struggling and defending the truth for 30 years, since the 1930s, and, of course, if one of them died, that would leave only one person to guard the whole destiny of the human race by concentrating on his particular version of what was accurate. And often, as I said, it was just foolish. From any perspective it didn't make any sense. It certainly was not about struggle against capitalism.

Very seldom did I hear these people talk about how they expected, if at all, to mobilize workers or to deal with migrants and so on. Besides, they were racist and that's another trip. On the other hand, whenever they had a program, when finally you heard that one of these so-called Trotskyites had a program, you heard that he was running for Parliament. It was a tremendous let-down, after all of this struggle for the truth, to hear that the only way to struggle for the truth was to run for the British Parliament and to lose their electoral deposit, of course, because nobody would take them seriously.

There was supposedly a new Left, literally [the people around] the journal *New Left Review* and to some extent around the London School of Economics. And from my brief meetings with some of them and my readings of their materials, my impression was that they tended to be very facile, within a tradition of attempting to be clever—the idea was who could put forth clever formulations. I was never convinced of any depth or of any seriousness of purpose among these people. In fact, I found a couple of them that I met to be upsetting even in the kinds of relationship one had with them. And there was always that latent racism, sometimes coming out in paternalism, sometimes coming out in hostile manifestations.

MOVING ON

So the position then was this: three years of struggle within my own terms, reading what I could of Marxism, doing a whole lot of writing and researching, and looking around British society. I also had a rare opportunity to see fascist Portugal in the course of my research. And that was another useful dimension—living there in that police state and having to go through that experience. I went across to Spain and found almost the same thing. And I came back to Britain to complete my writing of the dissertation with the understanding that I would attempt to incorporate elements of my reading and get out of that particular phase, that is, to conclude the work successfully and move on.

Much of these early years, therefore, from 1960 to 1966, were the years almost of pre-Marxian development. One, hopefully, was moving in that direction. It could have been dissipated easily if the opportunities had not presented themselves after 1966.

THE RETURN TO AFRICA

There were strange contradictions which one had to work with and work through. To get into the University of Dar es Salaam, I had to apply to the British Ministry of Overseas Development. They had a specific service, a university placement service, which advertised in England for positions all over Africa, from Nigeria, Ethiopia, Tanzania, Kenya, Zambia, etc. They interviewed you and it's to them rather than Dar es Salaam, for instance, that you sent your papers. And, of course, by and large what they were doing was recruiting the 90% expatriate staff that went out to Tanzania, or went out to Kenya or Nigeria, as the case might be.

But being in London, I had access to this service of the Ministry of Overseas Development like any other citizen of Great Britain. I put in my papers and I had my interview right there in London and I was selected. If I had stayed in the West Indies and applied to London, or applied directly to Tanzania, I have grave doubts as to how easy this procedure would have been. The imperial nexus was more important, and it facilitated my moving into Tanzania. I would have preferred to go to West Africa, which was my special area of research. But as I looked at West Africa, I couldn't see a place where it seemed to me that I could go and live and learn while teaching. Other than Guinea, which I'm eliminating for cultural and historical reasons, I didn't see that it would make much sense for me to go to Ibadan [Nigeria] or Accra [Ghana] at that time. All I would have gotten there would have been a good institution in the technical sense, [one] already known for the production of African history. But I don't think I could have learned anything from participation in the kind of politics being developed in Nigeria, or at that time in Ghana after Nkrumah. Hence the choice was to go to Tanzania.

My return to Africa was never an end in itself. It was always a means to an end, to me anyway. It was always with the understanding that I would return to the Caribbean or something that could go on there. I also felt that one of the ways in which one could mobilize was by picking up a certain amount of information within an experience on the African continent itself.

My first contract with the University of Dar es Salaam was just short of two academic years, and this was the more regular contract at that time, because I understood it to be my role to return to the University of the West Indies to teach African history and to relate to our people on the African question. Specifically, I was returning to the Caribbean by way of Africa. This is how I always saw it.

THE NEO-COLONIAL SITUATION

But it seems to me that assuming one says that one wants to return to Africa, or return to the Caribbean, the question is—return to what? I regard myself virtually as a product of a neo-colonial society as distinct from a colonial society. After 1953, in Guyana, the curious thing is that although we hated the British, it was very clear from then right up until 1964 when we got independence, that the issue was no longer just Guyanese versus the British. It was one set of Guyanese against another set of Guyanese. Likewise, it was one set of Trinidadians against another set. And in Jamaica, before independence, it was already a question of the progressive elements as opposed to the more conservative elements in the society. Therefore, in a sense, when I was in Jamaica in 1960, I would say that already my consciousness of West Indian society was not that we needed to fight the British but that we needed to fight the British, the Americans, and their indigenous lackeys. That I see as an anti-neo-colonial consciousness as distinct from a purely anti-colonial consciousness.

Now, that being so, a return to Africa in itself could never be sufficient to deal with the neo-colonial situation. If it was just colonialism, then perhaps I might have remained locked within a perception of Africa as undifferentiated. But I was aware of neo-colonialism. Neo-colonialism had already overthrown Nkrumah. It was not sufficient for me, or for anybody else, therefore, merely to say that one is interested in Africa, one is interested in things black, although that was certainly high on the agenda, because our society had not yet come to terms with the question of being black, or the question of being African. But that was not sufficient. Because there were black men in our society who were clearly the rulers to be, who were clearly being groomed to be the rulers. Therefore, one had to find a way of analyzing West Indian society to explain why those fellows were so foolish as to destroy the West Indian Federation; to explain why Eric Williams had said he would expel the Americans from Chauguramas and didn't; to explain why it was that Burnham was more accessible to the British and the Americans; and to explain why the CIA penetrated into Guyana. These things couldn't be glossed over merely by saying one must take a black or African position.

TANZANIA AND THE CRYSTALLIZATION OF NEW IDEAS

It was in Tanzania in 1967 that I believe I was afforded the opportunity to grow in conjunction with the total movement of a society, and to grow in conjunction with other comrades, younger and older, though mainly younger, who were also grappling for the same perspective on African history. And, therefore, it was a period of accelerated growth because many of the little things that didn't necessarily make much sense in the early period began to crystallize as one went to teach, to present a new formulation to students, and to address political questions in a very direct manner. Then the former reading was inadequate. One now had to read more. And then the new ideas were tested in day-to-day practice inside and outside the university.

I've always made the point that one's political contribution should come out of one's principal work activity, whatever that happens to be, insofar as it is possible. Presumably, if one is a factory worker, it is on the factory floor that one's politicization, one's consciousness, comes out in day-to-day struggle. And if I am an academic, and so long as I remain an academic, I must attempt to make the most important political input during those very many hours that I spend contributing to teaching or researching or whatever other aspects of academic life may come into play.

In looking at what it meant to be an academic in Tanzania for several years, I must provide some background. In Dar es Salaam, we were working within a new political context, that of a post-colonial society. But although we were working within a new university, it was not necessarily within a new ideological or academic tradition because the

University College of Dar es Salaam was, in the early days of the 1960s, an institution formed, like so many others, as a direct dependency of a large metropolitan institution. We, in the English-speaking ex-colonial world, are very familiar with this phenomenon.[4] You get the University of London establishing virtually a colonial out-house in the Caribbean called the University College of the West Indies, or in Nigeria called Ibadan University, or the University of East Africa in Kenya. The Italians had similar relationships with the semi-university institutions in Somalia and so on. The University of Dar es Salaam grew up, therefore, within this tradition of being an extension of a metropolitan academic institution, following the same norms, and very consciously, in fact, setting itself to measure up to what are called international standards, which, in effect, means the standards set by the parent institution.

In that situation, one has to bear in mind the development of struggle within the university and the development of struggle within the country. Inside the university we started at a severe disadvantage, insofar as the numbers of staff and faculty members and the numbers of students who had a prior revolutionary, or progressive commitment, were very small.[5] And one was also working within an adverse situation quantitatively as well as qualitatively. Both the academic program and the physical environment within the university—the administration, everything— were built and structured towards forcing one to behave

---

[4]See I.C.M. Maxwell, *Universities in Partnership: The Inter-University Council and the Growth of Higher Education in Developing Countries, 1946-70* (Edinburgh: Scottish Academic Press, 1980).

along certain orthodox, conventional, bourgeois academic lines.

THE ACADEMIC-POLITICAL STRUGGLE IN TANZANIA

Outside of the institution, however, real contradictions in Tanzanian society—class contradictions—between the producers in Tanzania and international capital were bringing about a series of changes which the world knows about in the form of the "Arusha Declaration" and subsequent documents, containing policies which the Tanzanian Government attempted to adopt and cement.[6] When these two things are taken together, struggle going on in the university and struggle going on outside of the university, someone who claims to be political, who recognizes a political responsibility towards political development on

---

[5]See Walter Rodney, "The Role of the University in Developing Africa," Public Lecture, Marrere Students' Guild, October 1970; also J.S. Saul, "Radicalism and the Hill," *East Africa Journal* 7 (December 1970): 27-30; I. Shivji, "Rodney and Student Struggles in Tanzania," Public Lecture, Walter Rodney Memorial Symposium, University of Dar es Salaam, 22 July 1980; and Bonaventure Swai, "Rodney on Scholarship and Activism, Part I," *Journal of African Marxists* 1 (November 1981): 31-43.

[6]See Walter Rodney, "The Arusha Declaration—Problems of Implementation," *Mbioni* (Kivukoni College, Dar es Salaam), August 1967; "Tanzanian Ujamaa and Scientific Socialism," *The African Review* 1 (1971): 61-76; "Comment on [Issa G.] Shivji's 'The Silent Class Struggle,'" in *Tanzania: The Silent Class Struggle* (Dar es Salaam: Tanzania Publishing House, 1972); "State Formation and Class Formation in Tanzania: Comment on Issa G. Shivji's "Tanzania: The Class Struggle Continues," *Maji-Maji* 11 (August 1973): 25-33; and "Class Contradictions in Tanzania," in Haroub Othman, ed., *The State in Tanzania* (London: Heinemann, 1979).

the part of the worker-producer masses, must, it seems to
me, enter into both of these activities and enter by way of
the academic struggle. That is to say, one's contribution to
the larger political struggle has to be made in terms of the
way that one might influence the evolution of the given
academic institution in which one is located.

That was the situation in Tanzania. Briefly, it meant that
we were able to teach and develop scientific socialist ideas,
bearing in mind when I say "we," I mean comrades like
myself, people of a like mind, because we were part of a
community and that was very important. It's extremely
difficult to really develop any ideas in isolation and the kind
of work that was coming out of Dar es Salaam had a certain
collective quality about it.[7] There were perhaps only a few
individuals, but nevertheless it was a community that was
operating. We had a degree of freedom which was greater
and remains greater than that which is accorded academics
in most parts of the Third World. That allowed us to pursue
scientific socialist ideas within a political framework that
was not necessarily supportive of those ideas, but was not
repressive in any overt sense. Indeed, in recent political
developments over the last three or four years, there was
the necessity on the part of progressive and Marxist
Tanzanians to indicate that their Marxism was not a factor
that could be used to disqualify them from participation in

---

[7]See Walter Rodney, "Education and Tanzanian Socialism,"
in I. Resnick, ed., *Tanzania: Revolution by Education* (London:
Longmans, 1968): 71-84 "Education in Africa and Contemporary
Tanzania," in *Education and Black Struggle: Notes from the
Colonized World* (Harvard Educational Review, 1974); also J.S.
Saul and Lionel Cliffe, eds., *Socialism in Tanzania*, 2 vols.
(Nairobi: East African Publishing House, 1972).

the national movement. There were reactionary elements who would have liked to have put forward interpretations that, by virtue of moving to scientific socialism, they had become communist infiltrators or something of this sort and that they were, therefore, against the national interest. But in Tanzania, unlike most African countries, this argument didn't carry much weight or hasn't carried much weight so far. Therefore no significant repression has been brought to bear against them.

My political role in that situation was fairly well-defined: to stay within the university walls, first and foremost, to develop and struggle at the level of ideas, to relate to the student population. For me, being a non-Tanzanian, it meant that I had to relate to the indigenous Tanzanians, indigenous intellectuals and students, within the university, and only secondarily to relate to Tanzanians outside the walls of the university. I draw that distinction.

Many people may say, well, it's a spurious distinction and it's part of the elitism of the university, or something of that sort. I don't think so. One must recognize certain limits in any given political situation: limits of culture, limits of one's legal and citizenship status, limits that come from the fact that we were speaking in the university in one language, which is English, and the people of Tanzania were speaking Swahili. And one must take all of those things into account, along with the historical record—the Tanzanian people, like other African people, had constantly been subjected to harangues from outside as part of cultural imperialism. It was necessary, therefore for these historical reasons, that we as progressive individuals (the majority of whom, indeed, initially were non-Tanzanians in the university), play our role mainly within the university. Tanzanians themselves, whether they had contact with the university or not, would play the major determining role outside of the university.

That was the situation for several years, for a total of nearly six years in fact (1967-1974), broken by my own brief return to Jamaica in 1968. At the end of that period, I felt that I personally had both contributed as much as I was likely to be able to contribute, given the constraints of the situation; and that I had probably learnt as much—it was a tremendous learning experience—as I could learn, given the constraints of the situation.

Let me concretize this by referring to something that was going on in Tanzania towards the end of my stay. The government initiated a policy called "decentralization." It stated that there was far too much concentration of the bureaucracy within the central government and the capital of Dar es Salaam, and that it should be spread out over the countryside to begin to develop fronts at all levels and in all regions of the country. Faced with a shortage of manpower, the government started to call upon university personnel to man some of these administrative posts.

My own reading of the situation was that initially they merely did this as a convenience: they were short of manpower. But it soon became clear that there could be a profound political implication to this, in the sense that it would draw the academic out from the university and involve him in the realm of real practice and *vice versa*. There could begin to be a movement, of sorts. However, by definition, a person who was taken from the university as a lecturer or a professor and carried to an outlying region to be a district development officer, or to some position within the political bureaucracy, had to be a Tanzanian.

We felt that there were elements within the bureaucracy, once it was clear to them that the university would be part of the manpower pool of resources which could be drawn upon, who would try to use "decentralization" as a weapon, as a means of splitting up progressive forces. But such a view comes in part from a twisted political stance, namely, that to be put out among the peasantry in the bush, to be sent to the sticks in other words, was the supreme penalty which a person could pay for falling out of line in one way or another, maybe politically, maybe in other respects. The British, in fact, had used this as a policy when they were in power: somebody who misbehaved, a colonial administrator who was white himself, would be sent into southern Tanzania, a place that was extremely cut off from the capital and from the amenities of what they called civilization. The Tanzanian government, to some extent, inherited this tendency to see such postings as almost specifically disciplinary. Clearly the university could be a target in some ways.

But whatever may have been the consciousness of the bureaucrats making this decision, the fact remains that the most progressive viewpoint was the one that understood that, wherever one happens to be, one can engage in progressive politics. And this was proven by a number of the comrades who were "decentralized," who in fact began to move out of their respective academic areas and to integrate their previous theoretical perceptions with the day-to-day administrative and mobilization tasks in a given region. This was strikingly illustrated by one comrade in particular who was a journalist, who went out into a very arid part of the country and was engaged in certain self-help programs of irrigation and the like.

The main thrust of my argument is that if I were a Tanzanian, perhaps I may have been "victimized" by some bureaucrat who would say, "let's get this fellow out into the bush. He may be talking too much. Let's see what he can do out there." And the idea may have been, indeed, to penalize the person so transferred. But for my purposes, in fact, this represents a step forward. It shows nonetheless the limitation of a non-Tanzanian, whether one is black or whether one is African, because Kenyans were also excluded in that regard. So were Ugandans, and so were Zambians.

I could have become a Tanzanian citizen, and indeed thought about it seriously. The question is, what does that really mean? You change your legal status, you become a new national and, therefore, hopefully you are open both to the advantages and disadvantages of being a national of that country. I say hopefully because there are times when people have changed their nationality and the government in existence or perhaps the succeeding government still treats them as beings apart. Because their citizenship was granted rather than being a matter of birth, it could be revoked.

That aside, it seems to me that in participating in a political situation, it is much more than a legal definition that makes one effective. It is more cultural, if you like. One must know that society, that environment. One must have a series of responses and reflexes that come from having lived a given experience. One must be able to share a joke because of a nuance in language and pronunciation. One must be able to go into the marketplace, in the case of Tanzania, and bargain in the Swahili manner without being perceived as an outsider.

Now, when one thinks of all of these factors, it's virtually a lifetime task to master that language and then to master the higher level of perception which normally goes into a culture. And I didn't believe that I could afford that. I believed that there was another culture from which I derived into which I could project myself with greater ease. Hence the return to the Caribbean.

THE NEED TO RETURN TO THE CARIBBEAN

As long as I remained in Tanzania as a non-Tanzanian, as a marginal participant in the political culture, then it followed that I couldn't change my role. I would just have to remain at the university. I was in a fixed political role and my own feeling was that to break beyond those boundaries it was necessary to return once more to the Caribbean. That is the background that explains where I'm at in the Caribbean and in Guyana today.

Most comrades in Tanzania were sympathetic to my leaving. These comrades with whom I had direct contact were mostly young Tanzanians, mostly within the university, teaching or researching or studying. A few of them were scattered here and there within the government services and so on, but they all were a functioning part of the Tanzanian political scene. They were members of TANU (Tanganyika African National Union) and the TANU Youth League. They were not a group apart in their own right except that they had an ideological consistency, a view and a way of interpreting the Tanzanian reality which made them different from other elements within TANU. A few people may have expressed surprise in the sense that if you're around for a fair length of time and you become part of a whole process, people begin to take your presence for granted. There were comrades and friends who were perfectly happy to extend to me that opportunity to participate indefinitely in their society, especially since, from our ideological perspective on the political left, internationalism completely eroded any elements of chauvinism that might otherwise have been present. Frankly, I found very little chauvinism or hostile Tanzanian nationalism while I was there, even from the right. Certainly, among the left there was no question about that.

At the same time they understood the argument that a revolution has to be made by people who are going to be grounded in that situation, who are going to stay there, who are going to make it part of their [lives].

There is really quite an amazing set of contradictions in Africa when you stop to ponder over it. Africa has moved away from colonialism and straight into the end of the 20th century. The problems the African people are facing are 20th century problems. We see on the African continent that the era is the era of neo-colonialism. We don't have to go through that long historical experience which the United States went through for a whole century in order to understand it. Because, in a way, their history is our history. Likewise, the history of Asia is our history.

So Africa has all these contradictions staring it in the face within just ten years after independence. In some cases the country becomes independent after these contradictions have already manifested themselves in other adjacent areas of Africa, as happened in the case of Guinea-Bissau and Angola. One's sense of what is to be done and where Africa is going must take into account these very many facets. I haven't even mentioned the problem of the Palestinians, which is virtually a North African problem and, in a sense, an African problem that is going to be another factor for change on the African scene.

At the same time, one must identify in certain situations the leading trends of change. Because, if we are correct in identifying them, then what obtains in a given place today is what will obtain tomorrow in another place—if we are correct in identifying the current of history. And for many years a few of us have been saying the highest form of struggle on the African continent is the armed struggle. Many of those who would have opposed this might have felt that this was at best a sort of romanticism, *i.e.*, awareness of revolutionary violence *per se* as being raised to a level of importance on a subjective basis. I don't think that that is true. Revolutionary violence itself is important in the sense in which Frantz Fanon analyzed it, as a necessary thing which people will seize when faced with the possibility and in the process transform their very personalities.[8]

However, my insistence on the preeminence and leading role of the armed struggle is not based on violence *per se*, but on the political dimension of the revolutionary violence. This dimension is the highest form of politics that exists on the African continent, because as a precondition of its success the armed liberation movements were required to develop their ideological perspectives. They were required to become very self-conscious about these perspectives and to ask themselves whether their old bourgeois ideology was sufficient to lead the struggle.

This must be taken very seriously. Even those of us who have claimed to take a revolutionary posture or a progressive posture have not always examined as carefully as we should the exact reasons why the liberation movements are in advance of other types of movements. I am suggesting that the reasons are because they are forced to make ideological reassessment, forced to mobilize the mass of the population, forced to engage in a politics of participation, and forced to create new state apparatuses over and above

---

[8]Frantz Fanon, *The Wretched of the Earth* (Harmondsworth, Middlesex: Penguin Books, 1967), Chapter I, "Concerning Violence."

what exists as alternatives to those of the capitalists and colonialists.

The constraints of circumstances meant that they could not have won the struggle otherwise. It is not a luxury, therefore, to engage in ideological debate. It is not merely an option as to whether to open ideological debate. It is not merely an option as to whether to open the struggle to allow the people to participate or not. Because if you don't allow them to participate, then there is no people's war and there is no victory. In all of these ways, I believe, the liberation movements represent the most important front within the varied developments taking place on the African continent today and their in-puts into questions of economic reorganization, questions of cultural reappraisal, etc., are likely to be very important in the immediate future.

More than that, the rest of Africa itself is affected by what goes on in the liberated zones. There are some areas in Africa in which the mass of the population, or elements within and connected with the mass, will probably more and more raise for themselves the issues of whether they can accept the present political situation or whether in fact the logic of contemporary Third World development doesn't push many more people into taking up arms as their only way of achieving true emancipation. In other words, it is not as simple as it used to be to think of armed struggle only as the struggle against colonial rule, as the struggle against alien minorities. More and more, it is going to be recognized as both internal to Africa and external to Africa simultaneously.

It is interesting, for instance, to find that there is a much wider appreciation today of the justice and validity of the Eritrean people's struggle. That struggle is halfway between a classic anti-colonial struggle and an African class war or civil war. It did not set out to be a class war within the same national state, so in that sense it is nationalist in form. Nevertheless, for years the Eritreans fought and were either ignored or condemned by other Africans because it seemed somehow to be heretical to support a movement which was against an already independent African state.

WHAT ERITREA STANDS FOR

But nowadays that is slowly dissolving and one finds that there is a fairly wide-spread acceptance today of what Eritrea stands for, in a general sense.[9] And when we examine this carefully we see that the Eritrean struggle has played a role in dismantling the old Ethiopian state in the same way as the Mozambican and Guinea-Bissau struggles played a role in dismantling the Portuguese state.[10] Ethiopian progressives today are making the Eritrean question a very central issue. The Ethiopian who is not Eritrean recognizes that his own society will only change at the point when it is prepared to recognize the fundamental justice of the Eritrean struggle and the need to do justice to the Eritrean people.

Here we see the armed struggle, in a different context, already showing the possibilities of change. This is not to say that there are no other levels of struggle. On the contrary, at the purely economic level African countries have been engaged in a number of experiments which day

---

[9]Cf. John Markakis, "No Longer a Hidden War: Recent Writings on the Eritrean Nationalist Struggle," *Journal of Modern African Studies* 19 (June 1981): 362-66.

[10]Cf. Edmond J. Keller, "The Revolutionary Transformation of Ethiopia's Twentieth-Century Bureaucratic Empire, *Journal of Modern African Studies* 19 (June 1981): 307-35.

by day are opening up new possibilities, if only sometimes by virtue of indicating a dead end—that a particular line of analysis or policy is bankrupt. There are very few people in Africa today, to be frank, however conservative (such as Houphouët-Boigny or Mobutu), who have not gone on record as denouncing United States and imperialist aid policies and aid givers as not really addressing themselves to the interests of the African people. If one compared that to statements made only five years ago, one would see that there is a considerable transformation.

Similarly, questions such as nationalization have been raised on the African continent and have been resolved quite swiftly when one takes into account that we've only had, at most, a decade and a half of independence. It is no longer taboo to talk about nationalization. This allows one to move to a new level of political and economic decision-making where you can say, "so we've nationalized, what does that mean? Has it given us control? Does it mean that the working people have any greater power in their own lives, etc.?" One can ask a new set of questions instead of being locked into arguing with people about whether an institution or enterprise should be nationalized or not.

The same applies to several other policies, for instance, dealing mainly with commodities. There was a time when it was necessary to make a point that we could and should demand more for our commodities in Africa. And strangely enough, there were leaders who were so reactionary that even this most obvious policy of getting together to demand more was something that took a lot of doing. But once you do it, you must confront the next stage. You get a somewhat higher price, but you pay more for the oil. Or you pay more for the tractors which you import. So you begin to ask yourself, now does this really make sense? But not only

that, you pay more for the food which you eat because the
United States and Canada and Australia will sell you the
food, while you sell them the raw materials.

I believe African political systems, even where they're
reactionary, are day by day being challenged by these
realities, and challenged in a way that they cannot avoid.[11]
You may run and dodge for a short while, but the process
and the speed of change on the African continent and on a
world scale today are so fast that it is very difficult for any
ruling class to hold up change for a whole era. That day has
gone.

Take "African socialism" that came and went. The old
form of "African socialism" has been wiped off the scene.
Nowadays people have to talk a little more progressively.
In Ethiopia, they have to talk about land reform, they have
to try and give it some substance. In my opinion, it's a
development of pseudo-socialism, but nevertheless there is
the constant drive of the realities of Africa, the material
realities of the untransformed social relations in Africa,
which cry out for some remedies. Those in power, those who
benefit from the system, cannot indefinitely keep the mass
of the population from raising these questions.

AFRICA ON THE MOVE

In that sense, therefore, we should recognize the motion
of history within Africa. It's not for me to postulate where
Africa should go. I believe it's more important that we
should understand where they *are* going, though obviously,

---

[11]See Walter Rodney, "Notes on Disengagement from Imperialism," *East African University Social Science Conference Papers*
(1970), and "Problems of Third World Development," *Ufahamu*
3 (Fall 1972): 27-47.

if we have a sense of direction, we ourselves as participants in that process will be trying to inflect it and aid it to go in a particular way because of our level of consciousness. But this is essentially an influence on an ongoing situation. If there wasn't that vitality in Africa, then, at best, we would be high-priests trying to say, "this is the way we pronounce things to be." I don't think that is the case now. I think Africa is on the move.

I've referred to Ethiopia before, and we must bear in mind the psychological importance of change in Ethiopia, a country which had almost epitomized the concept of non-change in Africa, and in the world virtually. The oldest surviving monarchy, a place where, whatever analysis was made, people always ended up by saying, "Well, it is Ethiopia. Things have always been that way. Things will always be that way in Ethiopia." The possibilities of change, therefore, are now opened up, not just in Ethiopia but within the continent as a whole.

It is a question of all things being profane, as it were. There is nothing that is so sacred anymore that it can't be overthrown on the African continent. And I think people have realised this. As I have moved around, and to the extent that I tried to read as much as possible about what is going on on the African continent, the early period of awe with independence is definitely passing away. People are making really searching statements and are demanding a change.

The armed liberation struggle, then, represents a certain very important trend for the future. Over and above its implications for the external enemies of Africa or the visible European enemies, we must understand it also has a potential in terms of an internal class struggle. Hence I mention Eritrea and Ethiopia. I don't want to go into details about places like Uganda, Zaire, or Chad, where I think there is a more authentic indigenous class struggle or revolutionary war which is likely to evolve. I merely wish to state that it is along those lines that a real possibility of change exists.

The armed liberation struggles started out as being anti-colonial but because of a sort of telescoping of stages, they moved to the forefront of struggle. They have advanced beyond the type of questions that are *not* being tackled even in the neo-colonial stage. They are raising and resolving questions that are *not* being raised and resolved in the so-called independent countries. I'll give a simple isolated example. Where has Paulo Freire's new *Pedagogy of the Oppressed* [New York: Herder and Herder, 1970], about the way one should teach and communicate in a Third World framework, been tried?[12] The answer is in Mozambique, in Angola, and not in Ivory Coast or in Chad. Even in Tanzania, where there has been a lot of attempted educational reform, they haven't broken through to that level as yet because the framework in which the whole thing is operating there was rather more static and sluggish than the framework in which the Mozambican brothers were operating.

The armed liberation struggle has become the highest form of struggle on the African continent, transcending not just anti-colonial struggle but dealing with actual revolu-

---

[12]See also Paulo Freire, *Education for Critical Consciousness* (New York: Seabury Press, 1973) and *Pedagogy in Process: The Letters to Guinea-Bissau* (New York: Seabury Press, 1978); and John L. Elias, *Conscientization and Deschooling: Freire's and Illich's Proposals for Reshaping Society* (Philadelphia: Westminster Press, 1976).

tionary transformation of peoples' lives. However, so long as these various struggles are intertwined on the same continent, nestling cheek by jowl, the impact of the armed struggle can't be shut out. My task is not to identify every possible struggle going on, but to identify the leading elements in struggle, so that this will indicate the possibilities of change. If we put Tanzania beside Kenya, it is important to note that the Tanzanians have said that one of the ways in which we will struggle is to prevent the creation of further class stratification in the countryside; we will struggle to build *ujamaa* villages. One could try to find out what is the struggle between squatters and landowners in Kenya, but it is more important to understand that ultimately such a struggle will obviously move to that higher plane which is the struggle to create collectivities in the countryside. That's why I've only identified the leading elements.

Obviously the popular struggle exists along a continuum: the struggle for land rights or a struggle for worker participation and the full-fledged national armed liberation movement are obviously stages or elements of a larger process. Now, certainly, if you call this continuum popular struggle in one instance and you call it peasant occupation in another instance, the armed struggle must engage each of these preceding processes if it is in fact to carry out the kind of mobilization that is necessary to wage armed struggle. And, therefore, there is a superficial confusion in a sense about popular struggle and spontaneous forms of resistance, *i.e.*, spontaneous uprisings, strikes, demonstrations, marches, take-overs. There is also a superficial distinction, but I think that at a deeper level popular struggle is continental wide and is in an embryonic stage in certain places and in a more advanced stage in others. There are class struggles that are going on everywhere which belie the claim of the world's neocolonial leaders that all is well.

I do not want to go into West Africa as a region, but Ghana being such a well-known case we can go back to it and understand what's happening there. You get, first of all, an advanced section of the petite bourgeoisie, with progressive nationalist views but not scientific socialist views, leading a mass movement out of colonialism to independence. The mass movement gets hijacked. The petite bourgeoisie takes control. False ideas, false consciousness aids this process and therefore, at best, we get some marginal reforms which allow the extensions of the petite bourgeoisie at the expense of the masses. I'm taking the most advanced situation and the most favorable from a nationalist perspective, which was what Ghana was. Then, at a certain point in this development the petite bourgeoisie decides that they want to seize power because the national leader is too committed to ideas about possibilities of change in the interest of the mass and in the interest of Africa. So, even though they wielded effective power, it was necessary to put the final blow on the Nkrumah regime by getting rid of Nkrumah himself. The military comes into power and they last a very short period of time really, an incredibly short period of time. They try to tell the people that everything that Nkrumah had said was false and that what they needed to do was now to go back in the opposite direction. But within a short while, sections within their own ranks had to resort to ousting them from their reactionary course and for completely failing to cope with the popular mood. There was a new version of Nkrumahism, so to speak, at least saying, we really are for Nkrumah; we will attempt to implement some of the things that he sought to put into practice.

Those changes cannot be understood without reference

to what I call the spontaneous struggle of the Ghanaian people expressed in a variety of ways, sometimes expressed simply at the level of their mood, sometimes expressed by the fact that suddenly you see in Kumasi people walking around with Nkrumah's photograph, which was supposedly banned. There are so many little ways in which the people indicate where they stand, and their rulers, in spite of having guns, have to take this into account. If there was not struggle, Ghana would have just gone backwards. But I'm saying that there *is* struggle. It has not concretized in that country in any new form. They don't have a new party. We don't even have a completely new type of military, because it is still the same old military in perhaps new uniforms, new epaulets, and so on. But there is a struggle going on. I do not know for sure where it is going to lead, though it seems to me that one can't ask for more than is in a given situation.

This is not attempting to evade the responsibility of seeing where the trends are going. But I can only see them where they are manifested sufficiently. In Tanzania, I could see a struggle around TANU as a political party in order to try to transform it. In Kenya, there is no such struggle around the KPU (Kenya People's Union) the ruling party. In Malawi, to the best of my knowledge, there is no struggle around a political party (there really virtually is none), and it is hard to know what is going on in that situation. But the continual efforts of our people, throughout the African continent, are constantly indicating that the ruling class is not comfortable. To be comfortable means they would not have found a need for repression. It would have been unnecessary for Mobutu to turn around having killed Lumumba and make Lumumba a national hero or to talk about authenticity, and, at the very least, to try and deal with where the masses are going by proclaiming what he calls Mobutuism or socialism. Here we see precisely, from the level of the petite bourgeoisie and the ruling strata, their attempts to manipulate the mass mood.

The inability to actually identify organizational structures created in a very clear way by the people in this or that country should not deter us from recognizing that the overall pattern of change is rapid and that we should therefore identify the leading elements of change.

The military are a segment of the petite bourgeoisie; whether they will be revolutionary, reactionary, or reformist depends upon other factors. They are just as much a social force as any other sector of the society, open to all the contradictions in the society, except that, in the final analysis, their institutional bias is still toward authoritarianism. That fact must be taken into account, because it means that, in the final analysis, the military is going to be anti-popular unless whatever they initiate is rapidly taken over by other forms of struggle. This is already proving to be the case in Somalia. They've begun to ask questions, such as, what about a political party, what about a vanguard party in a country that claims that it is for Marxism-Leninism? And the military replied, we will have a vanguard party before the end of 1974, for sure! But then the military has had this way of fixing dates.

In some instances, the military is more conducive to popular participation and popular struggle than in others, but I don't trust the military as a form of revolutionary advance. It may break loose a situation as in Ethiopia, but if they themselves are not swept away or carried upwards in that process, then their ultimate historical function will be to put the brakes on mass struggle, which is what they have already started to do in Ethiopia. They are already

doing the same thing in Somalia, too. They are a manifestation of class struggle, coming into existence because of the
objective class struggle, but then at a certain point putting
a rein on it, because they have the control of power. The
army is the military segment of the petite bourgeoisie for
the most part.

Part of my own response to what has gone on in Vietnam
is purely personal in its heightening of my awareness of the
absolute bestiality of capitalism and imperialism in this
epoch. Anyone who could see the record of imperialism in
Vietnam and have any faith in the capacity of this system
just to produce values in a society in which people can live
as human beings is being absurd. You have to deliberately
ignore the Vietnamese experience to have any confidence in
the humanizing capacities of this capitalist-imperialist
system. You'd have to ignore a lot of things, but you'd have
to start with the Vietnamese and completely blank that out
to tell yourself that you are living in a civilized world when
you live under capitalism and imperialism.

The response of the Vietnamese to all this has been a
truly poetic response. It's not surprising that Ho Chi Minh
was a poet. He got to the essence of things, because in my
own mind it is not a militaristic response that is dominant in
him. It's precisely a humanist response. The Vietnamese
proved to be superior human beings. They are a people that
have proved themselves in struggle to be superior to those
who had been sent to ravage their country or those who
were the local representatives.

I was very fortunate to meet a number of Vietnamese in
person in Dar es Salaam; both the Democratic Republic of
North Vietnam as well as the National Liberation Front
(later called the Provisional Revolutionary Government)
had representatives there, and it was a real pleasure to

come into contact with those Vietnamese individuals. It is an indication of their caliber that even these diplomatic representatives were truly revolutionary, a real achievement because the diplomatic set, irrespective of their social background, or the political background of their state, can often be extremely backward. The Vietnamese representation was of the finest caliber politically. Personally, in the humility of the people, their immediate warmth, one just recognized that one was dealing with something that was really outside of our immediate experience. Even in our struggle, sometimes I've stopped to think: we have a long way to go before we reach that level of achievement.

Our armed struggle has opened up certain possibilities, but it hasn't yet made us into Vietnamese. We don't yet have that capacity, which the Vietnamese demonstrated, of carrying the whole world on our shoulders for three or four decades. When one thinks back on this image of Colossus holding up the world, Colossus must have been a Vietnamese! They are the only people who are capable, singlehandedly, of holding up the march of imperialism, and we would be very proud to say we are going to become another Vietnam in southern Africa, because it would mean that we have mobilized men, women, and children to a level of dedication and participation, to an awareness of politics, their social roles, their cultural responsibilities and everything else, that singlemindedly they can defeat the most powerful imperialist nation in the world.

There is so much in the history of the Vietnamese people. Their tremendous capacity to deal with new technology, for example, is something which at present we haven't really given full attention to. Their continued commitment at all times to defend the Vietnamese culture allows them to talk about the Vietnamese past as a single continuum in which previous generations have made their contributions, and therefore they never lose sight of their essential historical link with their predecessors. They have steered clear of sterile international formulations like the Sino-Soviet dispute and stuck to their own guns and have attempted to maintain a posture that would not exacerbate international tensions within the world socialist community.

In one sense, if South Africa were to become another Vietnam, it would mean that we have another set of people operating at the level of the Vietnamese. In Mozambique, FRELIMO (Front for the Liberation of Mozambique) in a short time learned many lessons sometimes very directly from the Vietnamese, and it really is a major achievement that our people in Mozambique reached so far in that short period of time. But, even so, in southern Africa as a whole there is as yet no development of structures which could sustain what the Vietnamese sustained over the many years that they have done so, including the bombings and so on.

The other way of looking at it, and this is looking at it from outside, is what is the likely policy of American imperialism towards southern Africa? My own contention is that, probably assuming a minimum rationality of the imperialist system—this is sometimes in doubt but it is not as clearly to be thrown out of the window as their claim to humanity—while they have no concern for human life, they have a rational pursuit of their own interests. And in this rational pursuit, or at least this sporadically rational pursuit of their own interests, I believe that U.S. imperialism is *unlikely* to want to involve itself in a direct intervention in another Third World country. What we saw at the end of the Vietnamese War, or at the end of the war in Cambodia, is what the United States will hope to generalize in the rest of the neo-colonial territories, namely, the classic neo-colonial situation. "Asianize the war in Vietnam" was the cry and it failed. "Africanize exploitation" will be the cry in Africa. I'm not at all certain that it can be as easily defeated as was the case in Vietnam, because, in a way, they turned to the strategy too late in Vietnam. They tried to stem revolution when revolution was already under way, when the surging tide of the Vietnamese, Laotian, Cambodian peoples was too much for them to hold back.

In Africa, if the development of neo-colonialism and neo-colonial alliances and Africanization can proceed rapidly enough in this period, then presumably it could be a more effective barrier than was posed by the Thieus and the Lon Nols in Southeast Asia. In other words, if we envisage the near future and ask ourselves, what is the U.S. going to do *vis-à-vis* Zimbabwe, *vis-à-vis* Namibia, *vis-à-vis* South Africa, I feel that more and more they will tend towards supporting whatever option will promote the African petite bourgeoisie with whom they can establish alliances in lieu of the old alliances between themselves and the Portuguese on the one hand, or themselves and the white settlers on the other. There is still a commitment to the white government of South Africa and I believe that the U.S. imperialists will believe, correctly, that the white races in South Africa are, after all, their best guarantors for the continued extraction of surplus value; and that their best guarantors would be this committed European segment, which is partially already a national capitalist class, and which, if it isn't already a capitalist class, is so committed culturally to the maintenance of the exploitation of African labor that they are the best overseer class for imperialism in South Africa.

Nevertheless, it is possible to see marginal changes taking place and ultimately perhaps even more sweeping changes by which the old alliances are going to be transformed. They will be transformed in Zimbabwe, for instance, much more quickly than in the Republic of South Africa, because the white settler base is not strong enough for imperialism to lean on in Zimbabwe, and I can foresee within a reasonably short period of time that there will be a concerted effort to ensure that power is handed over in Zimbabwe to the "right Africans." This is my understanding of the detente. This is why Smith today is being forced to go to the conference table. In effect, the South Africans are telling Smith, stop this national war before it becomes a revolutionary war. Give power to some Africans who can deal as the Kenyans deal, as governments all over Africa deal with imperialism on a certain subordinated level.

That must surely be a first strategy. It makes more sense. It involves the U.S. in less complications to find a given African ruling class which will take over the task which formerly was in the hands of a white minority, or in the case of Angola, etc., in the hands of the Portuguese. I doubt whether they will succeed in Mozambique, while in Angola there is a real possibility, because of the divisions in the nationalist movement, that the U.S. could find client-sections of the Angolan petite bourgeoisie, such as Holden Roberto who has historically always been very close to imperialism. Roberto has never had any ideological differences with them, and one could easily find that a client class can be promoted. They might look even within the ranks of the MPLA (Popular Front for the Liberation of Angola) to pull out certain elements which are favorable.

That is a more enlightened strategy from their point of view than saying, we have some oil in Cabinda and these people are getting independent and we need to go in and protect that oil by sending in the marines. That really is old-fashioned and I doubt whether that will be a first line or even a second line of attack.

Connected with the creation of the client class there is also a policy of intervention in the political structures to either dismember them and hence make them less effective, or incorporate them in larger entities which are more susceptible to control from outside. This may appear contradictory but I'll indicate how this functions with certain examples. Dismemberment has always been a policy. If a country appears to be too strong, they start to talk about federalism. They did it in Nigeria. They tried it in Ghana and it failed. In a sense, they tried it in the old Congo, and it failed mainly because the U.S. ultimately had a vested interest in keeping the Congo centralized, since the U.S. saw that they could control the central government and it was better to keep it as one state. In Angola, there is still a possibility that they could try to either have a federal state or let Cabinda break off. In other words, let the oil-rich or the diamond-rich state, Luanda, break off from the rest and then concentrate on controlling those smaller states. That's one technique.

The other technique is that of using the larger entity to try and incorporate Angola with Zambia, with Botswana, etc., in a central or southern African common market in which the South Africans would play the leading role. The idea of detente thus also has an economic side to it. South Africa is saying after all, we can help you if you'll join the common market; you don't have to go and join the European Common Market, it's too far away; you join the South African common market and we will be the purchasers of your products and what have you.

In Africa there have been created certain zones of imperialism in which nowadays you'll find that, for instance,

Nigeria is controlling an area around the boundaries of Nigeria; Zaire is controlling an area around Zaire. Therefore, the U.S. doesn't have to be constantly looking over the shoulder of each general as he changes from day-to-day in any small African state. They just create the instability through imperialism, but they deal with one of these other established intermediaries, such as whoever governs the state of Nigeria and whoever governs the state of Zaire. In this sense, therefore, this dimension to imperialist policy will restrict them from contemplating, I think, armed force in the first instance.

Finally, however, the only guarantor of non-intervention in a direct military form would be the peoples of these countries and their relationship to the state. Is the situation after Vietnam still the same as it was before Vietnam? I have some doubts about that. Can the American state simply bring its armed forces to bear on the African continent without causing an explosion of the already developing anti-imperialist sentiments of the black people of this country? Can they get away with it by playing up racism and hoping to have the white sector of the population going with them? My feeling is that it is going to be extremely difficult, for it becomes more difficult as time goes on for the U.S. to manipulate. Cambodia and Laos were places that seemed rather far away and, as Lt. Calley said at one time, there weren't people there, only communists, things that you could kill. But now communists are assuming this human form and they are coming closer and closer to home. They have defeated imperialism in one area. When it crops up in Africa, I think the first major stumbling block will be the black population in this country. I don't care whether there are black congressmen, or whether there are black mayors, or whether they're supposed to be conservative or not, I really cannot see any black person in this country with any viability outside of a mental institution who could actually support the United States sending troops to intervene in Africa. And that is going to be a major contradiction. I know they won't come out and say that. And if there is some black mayor or congressman signing some silly document saying yes, the U.S. is right in going into South Africa, I believe he would put his life in physical jeopardy from some other brothers around. I don't think it's a simple task at all for the U.S. to just go and jump into Africa.

The question of how far the United States will be prepared to support the settlers or white indigenous capitalists in South Africa, how far external capital will see its interests being indissolubly linked to the interest of national white capital and the national petite bourgeoisie and the national white working class, that I'm not quite certain of. But I think that what the U.S. is already doing is trying to feel out what are the ultimate limits within which they can operate, in the sense that the untransformed situation is clearly too explosive. So it must be transformed in some measure. How far can it be transformed without changing its essence is one question. How much transformation is an indispensable minimum to get African cooperation, even petite bourgeoisie African cooperation, that is another question. And that is why there is a lot of running around from one capital to another, including U.S. ambassadors and emissaries moving from one place to another, trying as it were to exchange notes to see which particular baits will be acceptable to whom and so on. This is typical, trying to treat history as though it is the property of the ruling class, which will dispense however much of it they want to dispense at any given point in time. The lie is bound to come out. But one can't be just mechanistic and say it's going to collapse immediately. They could possibly give themselves a new lease on life for "x" number of years, however long that may be. That is a possibility. But ultimately, it is not so much being dragged down by their own allies: it is that imperialism is untenable.

THE CONSTRAINTS ON STRUGGLE

One can project that Africa will become even more significant as other areas of the world free themselves from the political hegemony of American imperialism. Certainly, with the demise and collapse of American imperialism in South-East Asia, you can see that almost inevitably U.S. imperialism wants to concentrate on the Indian Ocean and on Africa. Besides, there are real material benefits to be gained: the possibilities of more and more oil, the tremendous mineral resources of the whole of Central and Southern Africa, plus those which are being discovered and developed in other parts of the African continent. So we can see that there is operating the external constraint of imperialism, manifested through African governments and through the forms of penetration which are supervised by the modern multi-national corporations.

The internal constraints are largely derivative from the external ones, though not completely. These internal constraints result from class formation in Africa, where the class in power represents either a direct continuation of imperialist exploitation, serving as its compradors, or (and this is a more subtle development), its members represent themselves as a class and are prepared to modify or even confront imperialism on certain issues, but are not prepared to disestablish their political power. In other words, they want to perpetuate a given system of class formation which started in the colonial period. While some of them are actually prepared to try and cut some of the kinds of ties which initially nurtured them, certainly what they are not prepared to do is to break with themselves as the dominant class in African society. And that is what leads, at best, to a kind of political paternalism or very often to pseudo-socialism. That's a major internal constraint—the existence of this group which is consolidating itself around the state, by which means it controls state power.

There are other historical factors which are obvious constraints, such as the low level of technical resources, and the problems of health and education, and so on. But within the general dynamic of change, I still want to emphasize the rate of change and the rate at which problems are being confronted.

DEPENDENCY THEORY

Let me see if I can give some examples to illustrate this and let us look at the African intellectual class, for the sake of argument. Latin America has long had a very powerful intellectual elite because most Latin American territories were independent between 1800 and 1820 at the latest. So Latin America had 150 years, minimum, of a development in which these countries had an indigenous petite bourgeoisie and their own academic and intellectual class coming out of the old Spanish or Portuguese colonial tradition. And it took them precisely that 150 years to evolve towards the point at which a significant minority can today be described as a national intelligentsia who are trying to serve national purposes as distinct from being merely some sort of incubus placed there by Spain or by France or by Britain or whichever external European culture they depended upon. That was a long development that was necessary before Latin Americans could come to grips with themselves.

However, in the last 15 years, really more like 10 years, Latin American intellectuals in the social sciences have taken great pains to develop the concept of dependency.[13] I see dependency theory as very much a profound nationalist response. It is very often Marxist but not necessarily so. Many of the liberal-progressive Latin Americans, who might describe themselves as structuralists or by some other kind of description, believe in dependency theory and all that flows from it. They're coming to grips with the fact that they must have a set of ideas which will enable them to recover their national resources. This is what it boils down to. But it took them 150 years to arrive at that position.

In Africa, on the other hand, it has taken virtually less than five years before people started coming out of new universities, where they were discussing economic theory, and in a brief while they began to throw out the same kinds of concepts. True, they had the Latin American experience to learn from, but one must definitely point to the amazing speed with which this intellectual transformation is taking place in Africa. Today, if you look at the literature in and about Africa, you will see that the same dependency idea is

---

[13]The development of dependency theory can be traced to Raul Prebisch's seminal essay, *The Economic Development of Latin America and its Principal Problems* (Lake Success, United Nations, Department of Economic Affairs, 1950 - UN Publication 1950.II.G.2). The concept has been developed further by Celso Furtado, Theotonio dos Santos, Fernando Henrique Cardoso, and Andre Gunder Frank; cf. also James D. Cockcroft et al. *Modernization, Exploitation, and Dependency in Latin America* (New Brunswick, N.J.: Transaction Books, 1976).

rapidly becoming established as a normative position, exactly as it is in Latin America.[14] And few African intellectuals in the near future will be uninfluenced by it.

Thus, I am not unduly perturbed by the problems and the constraints on the struggle in Africa, because, as I said, they are very general to the Third World. What is more crucial is to try to understand the rate of the resolution of these contradictions and how sharply the contradictions are being posed.

Moreover, these are questions that can only be answered in relationship to our present time. A country like Haiti in the 19th century was lost in a political context that didn't afford it any opportunities for breaking through to a new level of organization in politics and social life. In a real sense, the whole of Latin America got trapped inside that era of the development of capitalism. But now we see young Africans asking questions in response to the contradictions of their own society and posing the questions correctly. And young Africans are offering solutions that definitely are in advance of anything that had gone before in the immediate post-independence period. So the last few years have been quite decisive in the evolution of struggle in Africa.

A second example to which I would draw attention is the way in which issues are being reconsidered very rapidly. That is always a testimony to the mobility of political situations. When things are static, people take the same old

---

[14]The principal exponents of dependency theory in Africa, in addition to Walter Rodney, are Samir Amin, Colin Leys, Claude Ake, and Timothy Shaw. For a critique of the African school, see Richard Sklar, "The Nature of Class Domination in Africa," *Journal of Modern African Studies* 17 (1979): 531-52.

issues and chew over them and present them in the same light, sometimes even for decades. When things are moving, however, yesterday's problems have to be yesterday's problems and you have to move on to something new. For instance, the question of nationalization was once regarded as the decisive revolutionary step for the progress and emancipation of Third World peoples. That was true in Nasser's time. In the last few years, nationalization has become common, but the moment that it became common you found a significant sector of young Africans immediately raising questions about its sufficiency, about its adequacy. They didn't simply lean back and say, we have done it, we have nationalized, we are therefore progressive. They started instead to say, now having nationalized, is it really true that we have advanced in ways that we expected to advance? They started to raise new questions about control, about management, about the class relations in production, and so on.

Examples like this can be multiplied. A very interesting one is the attitude to industrialization. As late as the 1950s and early 1960s, it was felt that so long as you could industrialize it was great, because the old colonial division of labor stopped us from industrializing. And so people began to industrialize. In Nigeria, Senegal, Ghana, and Kenya, for example, factories started to spring up. But again Africans were quick to perceive that industrialization in itself did not necessarily mean emancipation. On the contrary, they began to ask new and searching questions about the character of the industrialization: what is it all about, who owns, who controls, what do you actually produce? When you produce this, does it help the development of our economy? Does it make us more independent? These are really searching questions which in a sense are

WALTER RODNEY SPEAKS   69

the questions presented by our time. That is why I keep emphasizing this variable of the movement over time rather than trying to deal in absolutes.

NEW QUESTIONS
Our predicament at the present time throws up new questions. Neo-colonial man is asking a different set of questions than the old colonial man. Sometimes if a person gets trapped in a previous moment of history, you find it hard to carry on a conversation with him or her because they are still out to defend something that you're not against, but you're not with because it is no longer the relevant thing. Why should we get caught up in making tremendous tirades against the missionaries or saying the Europeans were terrible fellows, look at how these fellows exploited us? Why should we continually speak in this grand singular—the African is this and the European is the other? That was a formulation that was necessary at a particular point in time, when we were still within the whole identity crisis, when we were trying to evolve a peoplehood. But the moment we move beyond that, neo-colonial man can't talk about the Vietnamese in the singular or the African or the Guyanese, etc. We must look at real life.

In real life, Guyanese live in certain different ways, have contradictions among themselves, have a relationship with the rest of the world. We must try to deal with the resolution of those contradictions. And that is also the case in Africa.

I believe that Africans are showing a tremendous capacity in moving forward to cope with these problems. Very often, when you are in the situation, you tend to emphasize the other side. You tend to say, well, really, things are moving very slowly; if you look at Africa, you'll see that imperialism is triumphing—not is triumphing, but is triumphant, dominant, and still maintains its hegemony. For you don't want to get carried away by any romanticism concerning reformist solutions, etc.

But, at the same time, one must go back to this underlying movement of history and have confidence in the capacity of our own people: if they could have breached the gates of colonialism through their own effort, then it seems to me that they have brought into the neo-colonial period a capacity to breach the walls of imperialism today. And this is the kind of basic position from which I believe an analysis of the problem should start.

So, again, what I am talking about are trends. I'm not talking about fully realized phenomena. I'm talking about trends because it seems to me that the point of any political exercise is to recognize those trends—to recognize the seed before it becomes a tree, if you like. Of course, we may be mistaken and we may have recognized the seed that was sterile and it doesn't turn out to be anything. But I'm staking my analysis on the basis of what I feel are the critical trends. I see them developing, however slowly, at least at a rate that seems to be much faster than in the case of Latin America, which took 150 years to deal with the theory of dependency and we're taking ten years to deal with it.

CONTRADICTIONS AND STRUGGLE

But, if in our lifetime, the process could have gone that far, then where does it come from? It just doesn't come from the sky. It comes from the contradictions which people perceive in their own society. It comes from the continuation of struggle on the part of the masses which reveals the inadequacy of the new system. The new system just doesn't deliver any goods. What has the economy done for the vast majority of the African people? Has it raised the prices of their production? It has not. Has it offered more opportunity to people for meaningful work? It has not. Has it offered them the possibilities for real educational and cultural development on a broad scale? It has not.

Even where some degree of change has been brought about it, it has been lopsided and distorted. There has been no cohesive movement forward. The same is also true even in what appeared at one time to be so obvious a political question, namely, the need for the political unity of Africa. People have continued to be divided or even further subdivided into so-called tribal groups in the way that Fanon was the first to point out as directly dependent upon petit-bourgeois politics.[15]

It is out of those inadequacies that people have felt the need to say, we want to talk about *ujamaa* because we believe that this is a solution to the increasing impoverishment of large sections of Tanzania's rural population, while only a few get land and wealth. Then they go beyond that—when some others question whether *ujamaa* or nationalization is enough. It is because they can point to the fact that workers themselves express a dissatisfaction, an ongoing dissatisfaction, with the lack of change or betterment in their social situation.

QUESTION OF LAG

To the degree that there is a possible political lag, however, it is a lag between popular struggle, which is

---

[15]Fanon, *op. cit.*, Chapter 3, "The Pitfalls of National Consciousness."

going on all the time, and the perceptions of those who rationalize about the kinds of social solutions which could be pursued. If there is a lag, then it is in terms of a failure by people to find the organizational form to express their own grievances. If, for example, they started out in a trade union and that trade union has become emasculated and is the property of the petite bourgeoisie, then quite clearly either they are going to have to fight and struggle to get rid of that leadership or they're going to have to find another form of expressing themselves as workers. Therefore that becomes a real problem.

Yet, look at the way in which a supposedly backward people [in Southern Africa] who did not have any political participation in the colonial system, but who within the context of the liberation movements, in only ten years have seized the possibility—organizing themselves into an army; running their own schools; running their own health services; in fact organizing a new state. They are dealing with the question of women, youth, tribalism, etc., all within a specific organizational form of the armed struggle. For example, in Mozambique they spent some years wandering around petitioning to the United Nations, asking the Portuguese to do this, hoping to establish a party, hoping to establish a so-called tribal association, and those organizational forms failed. They then moved to higher and more successful forms, that is, the armed liberation struggle.

What other forms will evolve out of the African struggle, I can't really say because we're looking at some very embryonic trends. I don't know whether the trade unions will survive the way they are. All I can point to is that there is worker dissatisfaction. I would add as another possibility the question of worker control over production as distinct from bureaucratic control. It is one of those organizational trends which is likely to grow. But at the moment it is so embryonic on the African continent that I can't say that with any assurance.

THE WORKING CLASS MOVEMENT IN THE CARIBBEAN

The way that I would demonstrate this dialectic of struggle and change more consistently is by turning to the Caribbean. There we have a situation where, as C.L.R. James always has maintained, we have a most advanced working-class people. In a European formulation, somebody working in a rural setting is not considered to be advanced. But really our people have been operating within the aegis of capitalism for five hundred years, which is longer than the working class in the United States. We have been confronting capital, firstly on the slave plantation, and then subsequently on that same plantation after slavery. We have, in fact, a particular kind of material framework. It is not quite the same as a European capitalist framework, but the conditions of work are in effect capitalist and class alienating—that's the most important thing. The consciousness which springs from this is quite obviously a class consciousness and has been there for many decades and comes out sporadically in various kinds of revolts, the most recent and important of which were, of course, the period of labor revolts in the 1930s.

Given that background, if there is any lag at all between ideas and action, it is a lag between those who are manipulating the system and those who really understand it. Very often the people who are pushing ideas of transformation and emancipation are really only catching up with the majority of the population who have been suffering from the system and who understand that the system has not been operating in their interest. It didn't take the working class a long time to understand about neo-colonialism. Because in living their day-to-day lives they saw the continuity. They know that neo-colonialism hasn't meant any real change in their lives.

There may also be a lag between spontaneity and organization—that I would accept. Because a people understand their own immediate environment and are performing tasks which are necessary in that environment, it doesn't mean that they have the capacity and the tools to actually bring about radical change or overthrow that system. To work out the tools and the organizational tasks requires a whole political development which has not so far been fortified in the Caribbean.

So far we have been working within the orbit of petit-bourgeois organization. From the thirties and forties and up to the present time, the working class has attempted to use petit-bourgeois organization and petit-bourgeois ideology to address the problems of the working peoples. And this has not led them very far. Hence we do have a serious problem of creating the kinds of organizations which address themselves to working-class interests and working-class ideology. That is a critical lag which I perceive.

THE STRUGGLE IN GUYANA

At the present time in Guyana, I would say we have seen the depths to which a people can sink. But I would also say that we are probably seeing now the beginning of some recovery. Since the period of 1962-64, when the racial problem was politicized to the point that it became social violence (*i.e.*, racial and communal riots between Indians and Africans), since then, just over a decade ago, there has been no overt racial violence. But the hostility and antipathy of that period has obviously carried over.

In the wake of all this, one saw the tremendously divisive and explosive capacity of the racial groups when raised to a political level. I saw very little of it. But in 1960 we have seen a phase of electoral politics with people lining up on one ethnic side or another: the PPP, if one was Indian, and the PNC [People's National Congress] if one was African.

I recall very well, as late as 1960 or 1961, being very confused on the question of whether one went for the PPP or the PNC. And for those of us who were struggling for some clarity in order to take a progressive position, it was extremely difficult. Many who had joined the PPP as the better of a bad choice, as it were, actually had to leave the party. And, ultimately, because of these racial questions, a generation of us have actually stayed clear of the two dominant political parties.

The whole history of the 1960s was a history in which our political choices were fundamentally dictated not by any class position but by the ongoing race conflict. And it made it extremely difficult for any progressive, African or Indian, to intervene in the Guyanese situation. Because it was already so formed that the moment one intervened, one was doing so in a ready-made context of Indian vs. African.

In that respect, I was actually more comfortable in Jamaica, because there the confrontations were clear—class and ethnicity ran along the same lines. And when I was going through that phase in Jamaica of trying to formulate questions of struggle with brothers who had a nationalist consciousness [the results of which are to be found in *The Groundings With My Brothers*, London: Bogle-L'Ouverture Publishers, 1971], from time to time I did refer back to the Guyanese situation, trying to make it clear that the way in which one was using the word "black" in a West Indian context must of necessity embrace the majority of African and Indian populations. And the reason

I did that was because I knew that the word "black" could well be interpreted in a narrow sense to mean African and hence anti-Indian.

There was, in fact, some adverse response in Guyana to Black Power along these lines, to the extent that people perceived it as African and exclusive of Indian. Unfortunately, Brother Stokely Carmichael was in Guyana on one occasion—I wasn't there at the time—and he didn't help the situation very much by introducing what was essentially an alien, that is, a North American, conception of what race was about. Whatever he said, the common consensus when I returned to Guyana was that he had said Black Power is for African people. And that means African people must defend themselves against Indians—that the issue is that black people must fight for their own rights over and against all others, including Indians.

It did cause a considerable consternation because it came at a time, in 1970, when many serious young Guyanese were feeling for a solution that would resolve the racial issue. They were looking for some framework outside of both the PNC and the PPP, which would once more integrate black political activity, both African and Indian. And, therefore, that intervention by Stokely Carmichael was rather negative.

I always like to distinguish between the existence of ethnicities, whether they be called tribes or races, and the politicization of that ethnic factor. You can exist in different situations without being politicized, or certainly without being politicized into an act of confrontation. However, there is a little more to it in Guyana, and Trinidad, than just a case of ethnic groups. Many of the ethnic groups in African political systems did not necessarily have any conflicting interest in production, though some did. Some were actually, in fact, the remnants of feudal stratification.

But in Guyana there has been the problem that historically the working class has always been divided mainly because of the manipulation of the planter class. The Indians were introduced into the society specifically to counter and break the development of the black working-class movement that arose in opposition to conditions after the end of slavery. So it is not simply as though Africans and Indians co-existed without any relation one to the other. Economic competition between Africans and Indians was deliberately created within the construct of the old capitalist order.

Clearly, this competition could only be resolved by breaking with that type of production which required that there should always be a large surplus of unemployed. This is how the plantation system worked, for the existing African working class could be dealt with only on the basis of that large surplus of unemployed. Therefore, it was in the interest of the planters to bring large numbers of Indians to Guyana, not because there was a shortage of labor, but to create a surplus of labor that one could use for lowering the wage rate. In that sense, the Indian and African historical encounter took place within this context of contradictions with capital.[16] This was not necessarily the case with ethnic groups in Africa.

In Guyana within the African petite bourgeoisie, there is a very serious feeling of ethnic competition based on consciousness of the growth of an educated Indian group and the possibilities of this group superseding them in

---

[16]See Walter Rodney, *A History of the Guyanese Working People* (Baltimore, Md.: Johns Hopkins University Press, 1981).

posts which traditionally they have considered to be theirs in the old system. Therefore, in a sense what the new African-dominated Guyanese state is trying to do is to insure that some areas are closed off as preserves for the African section of the petite bourgeoisie, especially given the dominance of the Indian sector in mercantile activities and the like.

The ensuing competition is reflected today, in a way, more sharply at the level of the petite bourgeoisie than it is among the working class. In the sugar industry there is large unemployment. But the unemployment is largely Indian now. So it's no longer Indian versus African in that industry. It is now almost exclusively an Indian working class in sugar production. So there are no racial red-herrings to come in between themselves and management. They can understand the struggle for what it means. But at the level of the petite bourgeoisie there is much more of the racial manipulation by the state on both sides.

The African sector of the population, which in 1964 voted almost 100 percent for the present PNC government, certainly was involved in the racial riots. They were on the offensive against Indians, perpetuating communal acts of barbarity. Indians did the same and they backed the PPP. Now I think that we are looking in both communities at the process of political education that comes from ten years of experience and practice. African people in Guyana who look around them today recognize that their material and social and political condition has not advanced. Rather, in many cases, it may have declined in spite of the existence of this so-called African government. And, therefore, that must be a very important learning experience for them. They have to stop and ask themselves: what does this really mean when we say we have an African government? We have some people in power. The prime minister and most of the ministers are Africans. But this has not affected the reality of the lives of the African segment of the Guyanese population. Not the majority anyway. They can look around and see who among them have advanced and recognize that the system is one that gives opportunity to only the few.

For the Indian population, it is rather easier to maintain the racial interpretation because they can say, well, we as Indians are being excluded from power. There is corruption in the electoral system which has insured that the African minority retains power, although we are now the numerical majority in this situation. And many of them would just state that as an unqualified position. However, even among the Indian working people and some of the intellectuals, there is a growing awareness that though the petite bourgeoisie that dominates Guyana is largely African, it is not exclusively African. It is engaged in alliances with certain kinds of Indians—with Indian businessmen and the Indian petite bourgeoisie. And they can perceive, too, that ultimately the corruption of the government and its anti-people policy are not really benefiting the masses of the African people. Hence, there is a general awareness that is growing in the roots of both of these African and Indian communities that surely the time must come when the African and Indian people will organize around their interests as producers in the Guyanese society as distinct from pursuing this myth of racial superiority or racial subjugation.

I say that we're on the road back to a more healthy appreciation of politics, because the experience of the last few years is more and more convincing large sectors of the population that exploitation has little or nothing to do with whether one is African or Indian in the Guyanese context.

PART II

I have had a rare privilege of traveling around and living and working with black people in a lot of contexts. This has sensitized me to ways in which we need to understand the specificity of different situations. To talk about Pan-Africanism, to talk about international solidarity within the black world, whichever sector of the black world we live in, we have a series of responsibilities. One of the most important of our responsibilities is to define our own situation. A second responsibility is to present that definition to other parts of the black world, indeed, to the whole progressive world. A third responsibility, and I think this is in order of priority, is to help others in a different section of the black world to reflect upon their own specific experience.

The first priority is that we address ourselves to our own people—this is how we analyze where we're at. Secondly, we can say to other participants in a Third World struggle, here is the analysis, as we see it, of how we are going. Those people will take it and they will do with it what they see fit. But if they have a certain sense of internationalism, they will treat it very seriously. They will say, this is how a people see themselves. And only thirdly then am I in a position to say, from our particular standpoint, your struggle is moving in this direction, or this is how your analysis seems to me to be working, or in light of our experience here or there, we might want to question this or that aspect.

I think this should be said from the outset, particularly because there is a tendency within the black community at this time to expect a certain decisiveness and completeness in answers to any questions which they raise. People are searching for answers, but to be frank, sometimes searching for them in somewhat uncreative ways, because it really isn't creative to turn around to somebody else and ask what is *the* answer in that very global sense of the word.

There is a tendency to believe that somebody somewhere has the key, and I don't think anybody inside of this society or any one person or group has the key, least of all dare I put myself forward, coming from outside, as having the key. More than that, I'm not even coming from a revolutionary situation where we can say we have gone through this experience or we have triumphed, and on the basis of this practice we have a very important experience to summarize and to pass on to other brothers and sisters and comrades in struggle. So long as we remain locked in our own struggle, and it probably has still a very low level of organization and advance in the Caribbean, then I don't really feel free to speak with the kind of authority which people seem to expect sometimes. I say this in the hope that whatever I may comment on subsequently will be judged in light of this.

I also want to point out at this juncture how the differing patterns of development in various parts of the Third World can sometimes be confusing to people in other sections of the same Third World. If one doesn't understand it fully, one is going to fall into some serious over-generalizations. I have in mind this same question of race and class, and the way in which the debate is portrayed over here [in the U.S.], namely, race and class equal nationalism and socialism. Something of the same debate is going on throughout the Pan-African world, but not necessarily in the same form, or not arising out of the same historical conditions. Therefore, it would be unrealistic to expect the answers to be the same, or even the precise concerns to be the same in one area as in another.

The Mozambican and Angolan and Guinean revolutionaries, for instance, have a way of always insisting upon the priority of class over race, in a language that sounds rather similar to the language now being used in the United States, but the context is quite different, because they are not locked in a struggle of black against white. When they talk about race, or when they say a position should not be racist and that it should be class-oriented, more often than not what they have in mind are certain contradictions in their own society between the so-called mulattoes and the blacks. There may be some people in Angola who say that it is for the black Angolans and that mulattoes should be excluded; it's that kind of debate which often lies behind the pronouncements of Agostinho Neto or Samora Machel on the race-class question. While I don't want to enter into the debate, I think we must beware of being trapped into generalizations that are supposed to be valid for the whole of the Pan-African world, because, inasmuch as we share a history of a common exploitation and oppression, we do have many aspects of our contemporary predicament upon which, for the purpose of precise analysis, it does not help to generalize. We have to look at each specific history and the context in which certain concepts and terms originate.

More than that, there is also the problem that so long as one does not make a revolution, one tends to be continually at a disadvantage when facing up to other people who have made a revolution. It is very easy for [Amilcar] Cabral's view to be generalized because those views represent the views of a revolution, and a revolution that has succeeded, not just of a revolutionary.

Now, that being the case, one has to be very careful that what comes out of the last most successful revolution doesn't become the dictum for everybody else. This is not just within the Pan-African world. It tends to happen everywhere. The Russian Revolution becomes the dictum for the Chinese and then the Chinese Revolution becomes the dictum for the succeeding, and Cuba becomes the last word for Latin America. It can sometimes act as a constraint upon creativity. You only break with it when you make your own revolution. The black analysis in this country will speak authoritatively on behalf of black [American] people when we really make a revolution. Before that revolution is made, in any kind of international forum, such as the Sixth Pan-African Congress, black people in this country cannot really expect to have their positions respected. These initial clarifications should be borne in mind.

To exemplify the position I am advancing, Malcolm X as an individual and the Black Panthers as a group can be used. Malcolm X came at a certain point in the black nationalist revolution; it was at a very early point in the evolution of the civil rights movement, and Malcolm X was perceived by all for what he was, which was a representative of the left-wing of the nationalist movement at that time. In that current world scene he had to be respected for what he was saying. If one was simply to repeat what he was saying right now, in 1975, such repetition wouldn't have very much currency. People would say fine, but so what, where do we go from here? Malcolm X was respected as a nationalist leader, as one of the most advanced nationalists in this country, compared with everything else that was going on.

For the second group, the Black Panthers, there was in fact already beginning to arise the question of class as distinct from a racial emphasis in this country. But it was just in very non-specific terms. They were simply saying that it should be a class emphasis as opposed to a race emphasis. Yet that had an echo. It was immediately accepted on the left. It was found to be a very reasonable position, because really that is the position that derives from the experiences of Mozambique and Angola and Third World countries. But I am quite certain that the Afro-American delegation to the Sixth Pan-African Congress, including even the progressives, were not able to impose their view upon people who came with the stature of FRELIMO and the Cuban Revolution behind them. The Afro-Americans could not impose upon them any specificity of an analysis deriving from the United States. This came out in the very great reluctance that the left at the Congress had in accommodating any wording that even suggested that the category of race was viable. In the final communiqué, there were statements to the effect that Pan-Africanism does not recognize tribe or race or things of that sort. However, the race of black people in this country is not to be just dismissed like an ethnicity that is divisive inside an African country that you're trying to move to a higher level. We are a whole people. How could a Pan-African position say we don't recognize race?

It is because, when they say race, they have a different conception in their own minds. The only time that we could get this over to the international left—and I'm talking, first of all, about even the Third World international left, before we even consider the left of Britain or France or the Soviet Union—that talking about race is not some curious way of trying to bring in imperialism by the back door or something of that sort is by means of revolutionary action. The sheer weight of analysis will not by itself make that position become valid. As you make your revolution, the theory on which a practice was based has to be taken seriously. In my understanding of the international left, they will remain suspicious and prejudiced and biased against any position that attempts to grapple with the race question in a very fundamental way, because there are a real set of stereotypes in their response. They want to know if you're talking about "back to Africa" or they want to think that you're talking about Pan-Africanism rather than communism, in a kind of way that George Padmore used in the title of his book [*Pan-Africanism or Socialism?* New York: Anchor Books, 1972].

It is very difficult. I operated in the committee of the Six Pan-African Congress, and it was very difficult even to get them to sit down and listen carefully to a presentation which said that those of us in the Pan-African world, or in the black struggle, who have no problems with the Marxist approach [or] internationalism, and have them as our objective, feel that there are very peculiar problems inside the U.S. and that the people there must deal with the question of race, integrate it into their analysis and not just come up with the simplism that class is fundamental and that racism will disappear in the course of the class struggle. I don't think that the position would be accepted without some positive advances at a level of practice.

My contention is that even with the Cubans, when they speak of black/white or racial questions, naturally enough the main focus of their attention is Cuban society. You generalize on the basis of your own historical experience mainly, and they would be inclined to think that race means the same thing in Cuba as it means in the U.S.

In Cuba there was no problem for the white working class to ally with the black working class to make a revolution, because the white working class was also a colonized working class in a peripheral area of the metropole and its system of capitalist production. Whereas in the U.S., the white working class is an imperialist working class. I don't think that anybody who has lived outside of this context fully understands exactly what that means. I personally haven't lived with it. I'm trying to understand it by virtue of being here, many times talking to people who have lived here, who have been socialized within it, to understand why there is that basic difference. My response to whites and the behavior of whites in my own society are not quite the same thing as [my response to] the behavior of whites in this society. I don't think that this could be brought out for the Cubans or for any other people until we make some advances in struggle.

I don't think therefore it's just the question of analysis. Somebody like James Boggs has been talking about this sort of thing for a long time.[17] What tends to happen is that

[17]James Boggs, *The American Revolution: Page from a Negro Worker's Notebook* (New York: Monthly Review Press, 1963); *Racism and the Class Struggle* (New York: Monthly Review Press, 1970); James & Grace Lee Boggs, *Revolution and Evolution in the 20th Century* (New York: Monthly Review Press, 1975).

anybody who comes up with that position, but just as a position, is just likely to be put down. They look at that person and say, well, who is this, another so-called independent Marxist? Is it another Trotskyite? Is it another Padmore tendency? There is always this feeling, not only feeling but behavior, on the part of the dominant international left, to pigeonhole and categorize any position which comes from within a given country. It is never remedied until the people in that country are on the move.

I haven't found in this society any black organization that can be called in any sense a representative black organization, with a clear perception of where it is going. This is pretty well-known right now. I don't know, however, whether that is not asking too much in the middle of the chief imperialist society at the present time. The question of lag, of course, is a conception of time, and this temporal concept is important depending on how far and over what period of time we expect changes to be realized. If, for example, your time reference is just a matter of years and you say, there was a struggle up until 1969, from '69 to '75 there hasn't really been any struggle, I would say that I don't think that that is a very effective time-scale. That would be tying it to our own lifetime, to our own conception of the hours and the months passing by, and there is no way that we're going to impose our lives on history.

Our people have been engaged in a process in this society from slavery until the present. If we look at it that way, we would understand that the post-war changes in this society, like in any other part of the world, have been more rapid and more significant than any previous changes except the actual transition away from slavery itself. This is true on a world scale. Seeing it in a broad historical perspective, what we're talking about is the transition virtually from one historical era to another. We're trying to talk about trying to create a whole new society different from capitalist society. In that overall context, where legitimately one should be speaking in terms of centuries, sometimes epochs, certainly in terms of decades, I am not in the least perturbed if there seems to be a hiatus of two or three years in a given activity.

I would say that this overall historical movement certainly takes different directions. My feeling about the direction that it is taking now is that a number of people are trying to think through serious problems. I am not at all sure whether that is a lag compared to the fact that three years ago a number of people might have been setting fire to inner-city areas. I don't know that that action was any more of a struggle or a movement than people struggling with themselves to understand where they're at, which is what I think is going on right now.

Lots of things that were being done in the civil rights movement were very spontaneous. Most of them were historically positive. Most of them helped us to advance to the position that we are now at. Some things were not positive. But all of them must be taken as part of a generalized movement that is historically necessary. The fact is that, at the present moment, people are trying to deal with the historical weakness arising from the lack of a coherent ideology. It is because the question is now raised that everybody accepts that the need is great, and thus we should also understand the historical necessity behind the present searchings. It's not a historical aberration. It's not a gap. I think it's a response to a historical necessity.

I'll only talk about what I've actually seen, because I don't want to get into the grand formulation. What I have seen is that people are trying to deal with the question of where, at the ideological level, do we as a black people move? As far as I'm concerned, that's a more generalized debate, given that this is an imperialist center, than I know of going on presently in Britain among workers, than I know of in this country amongst white workers, than I know of in France amongst workers or even the intelligentsia. Here are a people that have come through a road of actual struggle for civil rights, not for socialism or anything else, who reached a certain cut-off point, and who, unlike the white working class, are asking fundamental questions about the reorganization of society and what does this mean at a level of theory.

This rather extensive debate which I have heard, which I have read, some parts of it in print before I came here, nonetheless has a number of limitations. I probably should concentrate on those rather than its strengths from the point of view of specific criticism. The first main criticism has to do with the way in which these questions are posed, because you resolve questions, obviously, depending on the way in which you pose the questions, how sharply you pose them, and how that all leads to a given conclusion. In this debate the question is sometimes, not always, but sometimes, posed very crudely as nationalism or socialism, and as race or class. The article with which many people will no doubt become more familiar, since it appeared in *The New York Times*, tended to say that there is this tremendous split between nationalists and the socialists. That is an over-simplification of the argument and not everybody, I would say perhaps not even a majority of people in the argument, actually say it is race rather than class, or it is nationalism rather than socialism. This is one form of raising the question, should it be this or that? I say that that doesn't strike me as being a particularly viable question to try to answer, because nationalism and socialism, almost by definition, if we just looked at the terms, are not mutually exclusive.

Nationalism is a struggle for a whole people. Socialism is either an ideology or a new stage of society. Nationalism could lead to socialism or it could lead to capitalism. It could incorporate bourgeois ideology or socialist ideology. So that these things are not antithetical. It would be better if we framed it that way. The debate would be more profitably carried on if people said, black people are of necessity engaged in a national struggle because that is the form of their struggle, and that what is critical is to understand whether or not the ideology and the objective of that struggle is socialist.

A more meaningful question perhaps, which a lot of brothers and sisters do ask, is assuming that nationalism and socialism are interrelated, assuming that race and class are interrelated, where does one put the emphasis? Are we really out to emphasize socialism or should we de-emphasize it as we move on? Should we place the emphasis analytically on race or should we place it on class? Which is the derivative of the other?

Those are somewhat more pointed questions, although even those questions sometimes can become sterile, especially when people engage in proof by means of what they call history. The discussion becomes whether race came before class, or class came before race. Assuming that race came before class, then racism must of necessity be the dominant factor, historically, that is. Or if it was capitalism which produced racism, then of necessity class becomes a dominant factor. I'm not so sure that I've helped very much either, because although I would argue very clearly that it was within the context of capitalism that racism developed as a system, which was to be developed systematically in turn by capitalism, I doubt whether one could proceed from that to say that therefore at the present time race must be subsidiary to class.

In fact, this doesn't even begin to define what is race and what is class in the society, because race and class are not just absolutes, they are concepts and categories that arise historically. Even if one arose historically before another, it doesn't resolve for us questions of analysis. Certainly, it does not resolve for us questions of strategy to say, since race came before class, therefore there should be no alliances with white folks. I don't see the link. These are considerations thrown in to link up processes which I don't see to be logically linked. A worse kind of historical argument is simply to say, look at the history of white/black alliances and you will see they always failed; therefore, the inference is that they will always fail. This is not a historical argument. This is just a circular argument. Perhaps it ought to be put in a geometry textbook: because it happened that way, therefore it will always happen in the same manner.

Those are the aspects of the debate that I would like to see axed, so that people can move on to more essentials, though I think that there are essential differences between the so-called nationalist and the so-called socialist approach. But to focus in on those differences, we need to stop involving ourselves in trying to prove the unprovable, as it were, such as that at the present time we can or cannot enter into so-called alliances with whites or what have you.

The debate is not just taking place inside the United States. It's taking place in Africa. It's taking place in the Caribbean and in Latin America, though not in precisely the same terms, but people are addressing themselves to these issues. It represents a challenge to bourgeois thought. However convoluted this main issue may appear, and I'll go on to make some criticisms about what passes for Marxism in the debate, I am not prepared to separate the debate from the movement of world history. I see it as a reflection of a generalized crisis of capitalism. Of necessity, because there is a real crisis out there, a crisis in Vietnam, a crisis in the economy, it must reflect itself in people's heads as a crisis, and force them to try and go beyond the limits of the theory within which they have been operating previously.

In this sense, I see the whole debate as definitely marking a step in the direction of the total emancipation process, one which has many facets. The consciously ideological facet was downplayed for a very long period in the history of the struggle. Ever since the 1920s, when theoretical issues were first raised there has been a tendency not to discuss ideology in any fundamental sense, that is, what is bourgeois ideology and how far are we participating in it and [to] what extent do we need to escape it? It is not sufficient simply that you state your ideology comes from calling yourself a black-power advocate, or calling yourself a nationalist. That is why people can run about talking about *the* ideology of black nationalism or *the* ideology of Pan-Africanism, as if Pan-Africanism itself is a pure ideology, or everyone who calls himself a Pan-Africanist has the same ideology.

The fact that today people are raising the question in the particular ideological form that they are is parallel to Africans challenging "African socialism," challenging the old bourgeois myths and deciding that there is, indeed, a class struggle in Africa and that it is necessary to under-stand it; that if we're to make change in Africa today, or in the Caribbean for that matter, it has to come through certain challenges to the petit-bourgeois structure. The phenomenon of the debate can't be explained purely on the basis of something internal to the United States. It is a manifestation of the international and total contradictions within the capitalist system.

Although there are many criticisms that I have of the character of the current debate, one must come out very clearly at the beginning and understand that the debate itself is another facet of the liberation movement, irrespective of the validity of the arguments or however misguided some people participating in it may be. I think this must be got very clearly, because there are some people who would like not to have a debate in actual fact, because the debate is raising questions about the nature of the capitalist system, opening up all kinds of things. The system is saying right now about Vietnam, please do not say anything, in another 50 years we might be able to understand it. Let us have a moratorium. It is like an archive saying it will be 50 years before you can look at the records; until then, please do not tell us anything about Vietnam, we don't want to know. It is important that a system such as this should not have any probing, and black people have also been a part of the larger society in that respect. Something which a number of black people [have] yet to painfully accept is that, however black you call yourself, you have also been a victim of the generalized structure of thought of white society. And one of the things that happened is that some areas of thought were just completely left out. Some things were taken for granted on the basis of certain bourgeois assumptions. So if those assumptions are being called into question today, that is part of our revolution.

In this debate, there are all kinds of college kids and people who a short time ago were wandering around in a bit of a daze. When they hear that so and so with a national reputation is in the debate, it is projected into their lives too and they begin to ask these same questions. I recognize this as a significant historical fact. This debate has been going on now for 18 months at the longest, putting it back to the end of the African Liberation Support Committee days. It started within a narrow focus initially. Very few people were engaged in it at that time. Now, for the first time since the 1920s, the debate has achieved a kind of magnitude in the black community. And, of course, it is not just the 1920s being repeated either, because people are talking about different issues, not just a repetition.

What I have been doing in this country, since I've been here, is to deal not with any organized movement, but just with college campuses all over the place. If I had [had] the opportunity, I would have liked to have dealt much more with organized movements, but I didn't. I haven't been pushing any questions at people. I've gone hither and thither and people have pushed these questions *at me*, people with faces that would be unrecognizable out there, not names, not stars, not leaders, just people who are in the classroom, mainly students. Last year only a few of them would have asked questions about Marxian analysis and its relevance. At the present time, however, most of these students ask these kinds of questions. I'm not concerned now about whether they take a position for or against. I'm concerned with the fact that people are beginning to consider it as something that you can discuss, whereas before it was nothing that you could discuss. The furthest that people went, from my own experience, in the sixties was a radical conception of themselves as a black people. These were the terms in which they conceptualized themselves. In effect, what people are now saying is that, in the search for a solution, we will remove all barriers to discussion and debate. They may ultimately not reach as far as I might hope that they would reach, but this represents qualitatively something different from what went before.

We will see in a short time whether the debate has had any importance or not. It might just fizzle out. We may be debating something that was a non-starter from the word go. But what I have perceived while I have been here, I have experienced very intensely. People are trying to grapple with new ideological parameters.

A seemingly peripheral issue, though I don't think it's all that peripheral, is the style of the debate, the manner in which it is conducted. From moving around and seeing the intensity sometimes, the near violence almost, where some people seem to line up on one side or another, I feel that the form has sometimes assumed more importance than the substance. I believe that the approach to the questions are unnecessarily antagonistic and project a number of other things that have nothing to do with the substance of the debate, such as people's historical role in the movement, if they're well known, and their ego and so on.

I can't really appeal to everybody involved in the debate and say, be cool and discuss this like friends. I would just be moralistic and it wouldn't make much sense. But one could say, to people who call themselves Marxists, one could speak to them in a different way. It seems to me that I could say to another Marxist that when one is carrying out a debate one has to approach it in a given way. One must have a certain discipline. One must understand that contradictions among the people are not the same thing as contradictions with the enemy. One must understand that the purpose of debate is not to alienate and intimidate. The purpose is not to force certain other people to retreat into their shells and hence to stagnate. But it is to get out there and let people understand the power of one's ideas and its relationship to their own lives and, at the same time, to be supremely confident that these ideas, if put forward in the clearest manner possible, will triumph against bourgeois ideas, assuming that the person to whom one is speaking doesn't have special class interests that will definitely tie him or her to an old set of ideas. I believe that I could say this to other black people who would consider themselves as Marxists. I don't know whether I have any right to say this to people who would call themselves nationalists, to say to them, look, you can't debate with this kind of vitriolic approach, and so on. If they want to debate it that way, really I don't have any basis of an appeal other than the purely moral one of saying that we are brothers.

But I think to another so-called Marxist it's more than a moral appeal. It's an injunction to such a person that progressive Marxists, revolutionaries, people seriously concerned with change, do not behave in a manner that is counter-productive. You don't just couch your arguments in such a way that makes people run in the other direction rather than come to listen to what you have to say.

I think that one can say to some of the people involved that the question of approach is critical and that this sort of putting a magnum to someone's head and telling them to choose for socialism is actually a counter-revolutionary approach. And then, too, there is a question of humility and discipline and study, which those of us who belong to a Marxist or professedly Marxist community have to understand. The humility should come from first of all confronting our own weaknesses. The moment you begin by confronting your own weaknesses you have to have a real humility, because you understand that your weaknesses are many. Even if you do score some advances in understanding, there are probably still so many other areas that are unclear to you that you have to take a rather less antagonistic view to others whom you believe are perhaps further behind and lacking clarification. With the humility on our own part goes the task, the self-imposed task, of more and more study, since to arrive at the position that we need to have a socialist society, we need to develop scientific socialist perspectives if we are to fully understand that approach.

Actually, my main admonition is the necessity for study and self-development, so that the profession of Marxism does not become an end in itself. Really, what does it mean to profess that one has taken up a Marxist world view? It only suggests that instead of using this tool, I prefer to use this other tool; instead of having this allegiance, I prefer to have this other allegiance; instead of serving one class, I wish to serve another class, which is the working-class interest of all communities. But having said that, one still has to go ahead, certainly as an academic, and as an intellectual, to make the analysis on the basis of utilizing the Marxist methodology, and on the basis of being intellectually accountable to the working people as distinct from being intellectually accountable to the bourgeoisie.

Do you see the differential here? If you change your categories, we're not talking now about the working classes as distinct from black people. There are not two sets of issues involved in being accountable to the working class on an ideological basis as distinct form being accountable to the bourgeoisie. Many people seem to think that as you move towards socialism you move out of the black community towards the working class, which, of course, is both black and white. These people don't seem to see it as moving out of an ideological framework which was accountable to the bourgeoisie, and which is essentially why very few blacks are in there, and towards an accountability to working people.

In any event, it is a task that requires study, that requires a sort of discipline that clearly could not have arisen in this society over the period of a couple of months in which this debate has been raging. There are obviously a number of older black Marxists who are extremely well-read and very well-disciplined, but for the most part these are not the ones who are engaged in the immediate debate. The latter are people who have just, as it were, heard about Marxism, and it does allow their critics to talk about "instant Marxists" and to cast derogatory remarks about them. Now many of these critics are not really bothered by the fact that these people are "instant Marxists"; they're really bothered by the fact that they *are* Marxists, that they are presuming to challenge the security which they have in their own minds, having been raised in a given intellectual tradition. To change from your world perspective is to deal with a lot of insecurity. A lot of people, not necessarily for class interests, in the black community will not want to move in that direction; and because they don't want to move in that direction they will pick on all the weaknesses of would-be Marxists, weaknesses like their attitude, like the fact that they haven't studied carefully or they don't know what they're talking about, and so on. To avoid that kind of trap, it becomes incumbent upon this would-be Marxist, this young person who is picking up the tools for the first time, to steep himself or herself in a certain kind of study. I don't like a word like neophyte, but really this is the stage that we're still at. We're at a stage of trying as neophytes to come to grips with a new world which had hitherto been closed to us very deliberately.

In the process of study, it is equally important that one should not merely study the classic Marxist texts. Marxism is not just a study of some classic texts written for some other situation. We should enter into the spirit of the analysis and be capable of applying it creatively to our own situation. Actually, here again, saying this is not particularly new. Marxist theorists, and even some of the youngsters today, will say, we want to be Marxists or we're Marxists and we will apply Marxism to our own objective conditions. The statement can be trotted out, but in practice very few of those individuals are engaged in the kind of work that is necessary for the application of scientific theory to our own society. Very few of them have an awareness of how misleading it can be to take an understanding of someone else's theory and just imagine that it can be projected on to your [situation].

For sure, I believe that those socialists within the nationalist movement in the Third World are usually the ones who have a greater capacity to carry out nationalist objectives than the so-called nationalists. But that aside, some of the people who call themselves nationalists, the conservative sector of the nationalist movement, can make a great deal of propaganda capital, polemical capital, out of the fact that these Marxist individuals are not deeply relating to the local internal situation. And because they don't relate to it, because they merely bring to it the thread of someone else's history, when they actually make a statement about what is going on in the United States or what is to be done, it can actually sound rather ludicrous. It not just fails to convince people, but it can be self-evidently absurd because it just does not address any part of the reality in the society.

I will cite one example. At a recent conference, an individual made an address on a topic about the current economic crisis in the black community. Essentially what that person did was to give an exposé of Chapter One of Volume One of Marx's *Capital*. This was all very fine, as far as the essential relations of capital and the alienation of labor and surplus value and so on were concerned, but he didn't say anything about black people except by inference. At the end of it all, he sort of suggested that what he had just laid down, which was Marx's understanding of the development of capitalism in the then most highly developed capitalist state, namely Britain, and which is what Marx saw in Manchester, was what he, too, had just gone out and seen in Detroit or in New York. This is so patently absurd that if the analysis can't be transferred in some better way, it is going to reinforce the impression that it is irrelevant. And for many people, some I think because they are against it anyway, but some because they have not been exposed to anything else, they will look at such a caricature and they will say, what is going on? What is this fellow talking about? Oh, the Marxists again, here they are! Then they'll start to say, well the next thing he will tell us is we must have an alliance with white labor, we have had that before, and he's probably going to ask us to join the Communist party. We also had that before. So there is always that danger of cynicism, of *déjà vu*, coming into play.

It's our responsibility to avoid falling into that kind of trap. But again, I don't think I could say to the nationalist, please be cool and understand that the brother is just entering into the discipline, he will get around to applying it to society, and so on. The reason is that it may not be in the class interest of the particular person who calls himself a nationalist. But when you're working amongst black people, a vast majority of whom are potentially capable of internalizing a socialist ideology, we must assume that the responsibility is ours to demonstrate its relevance. Let us be sure to let people participate in a real debate about what is going on in society. For what it is worth, I feel that is the kind of admonition which I would give to at least some of the participants in the debate. They need to be far more careful to avoid alienating people by even seeming to be, and very often actually being, the bringers of an alien analysis. Or not even an analysis, since the example I have been referring to is a non-analysis. It's really a fixed position substituting for an analysis of the society.

I hesitate to be particularly hard on anybody involved in the current debate, because I'm not sure that even if I were part of it, and living here and studying it, I could be very much better with respect to answers. Though hopefully, I could try to clarify some questions a little better.

What the uniqueness of the black situation means, to look at it programatically, is that at this moment it is extremely difficult for any progressive black leader to operate outside of the boundaries of the black community. At this particular time, for this era, I believe that our history imposes upon a black Marxist the necessity to operate almost exclusively, certainly essentially, within the black community. Now I know that will be likely to sound heretical to many Marxists because they will say, but surely your constituency is the working class and you should therefore transcend, rather than be a prisoner of, the racial divisions within the class, because these racial divisions are essentially divisions at the subjective level of consciousness. This is how the traditional argument will go, but I'm not at all convinced about that. They might be right but I find it rather peculiar, and I believe that a number of mistaken strategies derive from taking the racial divisions merely as subjective and therefore as something that you break down merely by speaking to the white worker and by exposing him to a superior logic. I believe that superior logic works only where there is no rooted class interest. Perhaps I should go further and say, where there is no historical privilege, because while there may not be a sharp class difference between a black worker and a white worker, there are certainly differences of historical privilege in all respects—culturally, politically, economically, and in terms of social mobility.

Our whole debate about the character of this differentiation is predicated upon a terminology that may be inadequate even to deal with this situation. For us at this point in time, before we actually do the analysis, all things must be open-ended. This is not an attempt to be ambivalent or not to take a definite position, it is just to recognize that if you're dealing with a new situation, then very often you need a whole new terminology in order to apply the Marxist methodology to a completely new situation.

For the sake of argument, though it is not quite exact, I will give a parallel that will help to show the direction of my thought. For Marx, it was sufficient to make a distinction between the landlord and the peasant in feudal society and to talk about the peasants, the workers, and the capitalist as feudalism declined and as capitalism developed. In some of his essays and writings, Engels had cause to go a little more deeply into the peasantry, but not very deep. It became Lenin's task, concentrating on a different society, namely Russia, and its different history, to start talking seriously about differentiations within the peasantry, so that he had to utilize terms like the rich peasantry, the middle peasantry, and the poor peasantry. Indeed, in China that differentiation became even more critical. A whole strategy in China was based upon not looking at peasants as a whole, *i.e.*, peasants versus the landlord class or the capitalist class, but working out an understanding of the relations between rich and poor peasant or middle and poor peasant. Now nobody said that the concept of the peasantry had to be thrown out of the window. Similarly, it seems to me, without throwing out of the window the concept of the proletariat, surely the difference between the black and white proletariat is at least as significant conceptually as the difference between middle peasant and poor peasant, which very often was a small difference that nevertheless was politically important. The differences between the white working class as a whole and the black working class as a whole must surely be more politically important than that between a poor and a middle or even a rich and a middle peasant.

Yet we seem stuck. The term proletariat has a magic significance. Starting with the predilection that class is important and that therefore, somehow the use of the word proletariat is fundamental, it seems we are only prepared to make, at best, some sort of peripheral concessions on the basis of this initial assumption. Very few people seem to be willing to do the work in some ways James Boggs has attempted to do, of looking at this working class along the lines of race and the divisions inside of it historically and seeing that this embodies real differences.

At the present moment, to the extent that we want to say that there are in fact, two different classes, surely we must open up our perspectives. This is one of the things that I feel is not being done sufficiently. In this sense, it's not so much the neophytes that I'm concerned with now. Some people who have been talking about Marxism for some while and who have a grasp of the theory, in my opinion, don't seem to want to break loose from previous categories. This is strange, because in the Third World currently analysts are dealing with whatever situation comes up. In Africa and Latin America, people are almost every day sometimes just coining new terms. Perhaps that goes a little bit too far, but at least that speaks to their willingness to recognize that when new phenomena appear on the scene, you must recognize them to be new and not imagine that you're simply speaking of an extension of something that was going on in the 19th century. Clearly there are a lot of new phenomena since that time. The phenomena of a race encrusted within a class in the particular way that the black working class is situated and functions is definitely not found anywhere else. I don't know whether that terminology itself is even adequate to the analysis at the present time.

It is true that the model of black people as an "internal colony"[18] has been used for quite some time in the United States, but it has limitations. It hasn't gone in the direction of really explaining the characteristics of a working class in a colony. Are those characteristics represented in the United States among black people? I don't think that question ever really came out clearly in the use of this "internal colony" model. Indeed, it's only now that people are beginning to look more closely at the specific character-istics of the working class in the colony compared to the metropole, recognizing the differences in wage rates, organizational structure and power, access to the state,

---

[18] Robert Blauner, "Internal Colonialism and Ghetto Revolt," *Social Problems* 16 (Spring 1969): 393-408; Charles V. Hamilton, "Conflict, Race and System-Transformation in the United States," *Journal of International Affairs* 23 (1969): 106-108.

and cultural and racial perception. All these differences distinguish a capitalist worker or a worker in the capitalist metropole from a worker in the peripheral areas of the Third World.

If we looked at those differences, we might want to ask ourselves whether we can perceive similar kinds of differences within the history of the black working people here in the U.S. Blacks, in fact, have had different degrees of access to the means of production compared with white workers. While white workers could get wage employment, black workers after slavery became quasi-free labor under the regime of the southern sharecropping system. While white workers could get jobs, black workers formed the majority of the unemployed pool. I was recently participating in a discussion where the brother, who was a serious Marxist, took a very clear anti-imperialist position, but he was saying nonetheless that the difference between white workers and black workers boiled down to about $100 a year in income. I found that a little worrying, that a serious person should reduce the situation to this abstraction of $100 a year. What has happened to all this history? Do you mean that if I went out there and if I had the power to distribute $100 a year more to every black worker, I would have eliminated the problem? Surely it can't be reduced just to that kind of very elementary variable.

We shall need to push for much more serious work to examine what may be the uniqueness of the American situation. However, I think that what really happens is this: Ordinary black people know the uniqueness that exists and if you come up with a theory that says it doesn't exist, then you're joking, because your theory is irrelevant to how they see themselves, false consciousness or no false consciousness. No people could be so falsely conscious of black people living in this society as not to know that the whole range of choices in this society is not predicated merely upon the fact that a black worker earns $100 less than a white worker.

Although these thoughts are more doubts and questions than they are answers, the suggestions come to me from looking at my own society. In the Caribbean we, too, have to grapple with uniqueness. We have to ask what are the specific characteristics of the petite bourgeoisie as a class, as it develops around the state. That's not a question which Europeans ask because that is not their situation. We still have a large peasantry. Do we treat them as petty commodity producers and as a consequence as members of the petite bourgeoisie, or do we see them as part of the working people, the producers in our country? What do we do with the large number of unemployed? Thirty-three per cent of our population is unemployed. Do we call them "lumpen proletariat" and with all that that implies—that they're outside the working class, that they are even in some ways anti-social—or should we understand that this is a fundamental part of the development of capitalism in our society? It is part of the thrust of capitalism to keep our working people from even having the right to work.

We have to move through some of these kinds of ideological and analytical problems ourselves. More than that, we also have to grapple with things are are not true over here in the United States. Over here it's Marxism vs bourgeois thought really, because I don't think it's vs nationalism. But in our society, in some sectors, we are already moving to a stage where the petite bourgeoisie says, we're socialist, we're Marxists. What do you do in that kind of context? We in the Caribbean are now beginning to get over the differences between pseudo-socialism and real socialism.

Some of the Europeans have also had this problem. Marxism has appealed to a number of European intellectuals and they use it just as any other tool, exactly as they would a theory from Weber or someone else, and a number of other European Marxists have arisen to directly contradict this. They say to these intellectuals, you can't read Marx and read him to be liberal, you must understand that there is a revolutionary dimension, there is a class dimension to his thought.

So each situation raises different kinds of questions. Ultimately, the real problem comes: How do these patterns of thought relate to the ongoing movement in a particular society? How do they relate to organization and practice? Among most Marxists, this is a big thing. Again, everybody will agree, theory cannot be separated from practice, theory and practice are inseparable, practice depends upon theory and vice versa. These are almost clichés within a Marxist context. But actually carrying it out is of a different order completely, and more often than not there are serious contradictions between what people say and what they do.

A group, for example, might begin by denouncing Stalinism or denouncing revisionism. But then you look at the social practice in their own organization and it is more Stalinist or it's more revisionist. In other words, people don't seem to understand that you're not just denouncing theory but you are trying to work out an alternative way of doing things. And because they don't make that connection to their own lives, they can go ahead denouncing Stalinism and revisionism and still act in precisely the same fashion which gave rise to phenomena of that type.

In this country, this is a real problem because, after all, the U.S. as a whole, not just the black community, suffers from the lack of a ready-made context for revolutionary practice. The reason is that if you have a theory about revolutionary change, but the whole world sees that it is not yet right for the revolutionary transformation in your own society, you are just hung out there; you are isolated from any real practice. This is particularly so for the white left, because traditionally a practice would have to be within the working class or at least among the most radical sectors of the intelligentsia. In this country, the whole working class base has been divided up between black and white. The race question has divided them. White Marxists, although they have never theoretically accepted it, of course, have always in practice recognized the leading role of the black working class, because that's the only place they've gone to try and engage in some practice. You can't go to Mr. [George] Meany's union [AFL-CIO] to practice any socialism. There is no possibility within that structure, as it is presently, of engaging in day-to-day worker education and the like, because the few who have tried it have been sucked into a meaningless pro-imperialist trade unionist type of politics that [has] nothing to do with working class power. And this is what socialism is about. The black intellectual, or the black activist, is, to my mind, better off than the white activist or white intellectual, but not necessarily in an ideal position either. I think that there is an ongoing black struggle to which black intellectuals, black socialists, black revolutionaries can relate in a way that could help them to strengthen their theory in an image of practice.

But it remains difficult. In Africa I feel that chances are greater of that practice. In the Caribbean I believe the chances are also greater. I don't think anybody can really come along and say the Caribbean people are not ready for revolutionary action, because, on the contrary, we see it time and time again. Right now in Trinidad you see society in turmoil. Our people are out there. There is lots of scope for relating ideas to the movement of the masses. And that is our task.

I hope that we can fulfill the task in the Caribbean and thereby offer the basis for some kind of fraternal alliance with struggle inside the United States. Because, when one thinks of Pan-Africanism, the Caribbean after all is much closer than Africa. The slow development of nationalist struggle in the Caribbean has perhaps obscured the fact that there is real potential for an alliance. The example of Cuba precisely shows what are the possibilities. Cuba was not even within the language orbit, nor the shared culture which Afro-Americans and black people in the English-speaking Caribbean have. Yet Cuba could have begun to make an important impact here in the U.S., just as we benefited a great deal in the sixties from the currents which came from the nationalist struggle in this country among black people in the Caribbean.

Similarly, any breakthrough in the English-speaking Caribbean, by which I mean a socialist breakthrough, *i.e.*, a new ordering of society on an egalitarian basis, in Trinidad or Jamaica or Guyana would perhaps add another dimension to the struggle here. Again I must be careful. *Our* practice will not be *your* practice. People here would still have to work out the specificity of their own situation, but being closer and by means of indicating the overall trend of world history, anything occurring in the Caribbean along socialist lines would, I feel, be of real significance to the struggle here.

An idea that has been gaining prominence in my mind as I have moved around from one institution to another in this country is the idea of intellectual struggle. All these huge concrete and glass buildings rising up into the sky are a little different from my normal environment. It does strike me, at any rate (I'm not sure about people who live under it permanently), as representing architecturally the power of the ruling class. These institutions are powerful; we can't underestimate their power. The United States as a whole is powerful. It must have appeared that way to the Vietnamese. Portugal must have appeared in the same way to the Mozambican and the Guinean people that this 30-story building appears to me, as I come onto one of these university campuses, and I stand up and I stare upwards and I see this tremendous structure which I know doesn't belong to us. Everybody knows it doesn't belong to us.

Black people are here in these institutions as a part of the development of black struggle, but only as a concession designed to incorporate us within the structure. I use the term "guerrilla intellectual" to come to grips with the initial imbalance of power in the context of academic learning. Going beyond the symbolism of the building, I'm thinking also of the books, the references, the theoretical assumptions, and the entire ideological underpinnings of what we have to learn in every single discipline. Once you understand the power that all this represents, then you have to recognize that your struggle must be based on an honest awareness of the initial disparity. And that's how the guerrilla operates. The guerrilla starts out by saying, the enemy has all and we have nothing in terms of weapons, but we have a lot of other things. We start to make and invent what we actually have, and we use that strength to transform the actual logistical position over a period of time into one where we call the tune and ultimately carry the battle to the enemy. This is the symbolism, if you like, behind the use of the term "guerrilla intellectual."

What would be new about it? First of all, I think that many of us from the Third World, and I think that black people in this country are a part of this, felt that when we went into a given institution we were going there to become legitimate. The institution gave us legitimacy. The institutions were legitimate in their own right. The activity in which we were engaged was considered legitimate. I'm arguing for a transformation of this and an awareness that the legitimacy of the institution is a specific class legitimacy, and we do not want to accept that legitimacy. We want to find ways of breaking with it, so that whatever we may get in that environment we must get through struggle, and not because it is being given to us to legitimize us.

It's been pointed out to me in a discussion on these issues that black students have always taken this attitude, and that black people in white institutions have always understood that these weren't our institutions and we were just there for what we could get out of them. But I don't accept that. This may be true but only in the sense, to which I referred earlier, that many black students felt that what we wanted to get out of them was the credential for moving around with a minimum of effort. One rejected so-called white thought, white institutions, and white learning, and one did not wage a struggle against it on its own terms. The guerrilla does that. The guerrilla wages a struggle; he or she wages a struggle for that terrain, not initially by confronting an army but their task is to occupy the terrain. Their task is to free the whole structure. And I don't know that black people did, in fact, enter these institutions in that way.

A criticism that was raised earlier along these lines is that surely, after all, the struggle is outside and not within these institutions. These institutions are just an epiphenom- ana as far as black peoples' participation is concerned. I say no. I say this is running away from the responsibility of the intellectual and academic class. The major and first responsibility of the intellectual is to struggle over ideas. We didn't create the artificial distinction between mental and manual labor but it is there, and if it is to be transcended, it isn't simply to be transcended by a so-called progressive intellectual going out to become a manual laborer. It is to be transcended by breaking the pattern of society that en- trenches such a distinction. Therefore the first level of struggle for the intellectual is in his own sphere of operation.

I have the greatest respect for those intellectuals who have taken up the gun, but one must also recognize there are severe limitations in that. There are not very many who have done it very successfully or had the equipment to do it successfuly. It is not everybody who will become a Che Guevara. That kind of image could even become destructive.

So the "guerrilla intellectual" is one who is participating in this whole struggle for transformation within his own orbit. His or her task is to operate within the aegis of the institution and the structure and to take from it and to transform it over time. The transformation is extremely difficult but taking from it means taking the best that it has to offer which is, in a sense, expropriating bourgeois knowledge. The bourgeoisie have already expropriated so much from the laboring population. They have the facilities and the possibilities for the elaboration of knowledge, which they use in a peculiar kind of way. We have to find ways of mastering that knowledge from a different perspective. This is where the class question comes in, not by running in there and thinking that our metaphysics are better than their metaphysics, but by understanding that there is a science in the analysis of society and that we should utilize the opportunity within these particular structures of learning and ideas to subvert the intention of the capitalists to reproduce us as members of their service class. The petite bourgeoisie is a service class, a managerial class, with respect to ideas and administration. It is that struggle to which I am trying to refer when I use that concept of the "guerrilla intellectual."

At the same time, we need a more positive orientation than simply reacting to white scholarship. Whether it be in black schools or in white schools or independent institutions (and that is the whole meaning of The Institute of the Black World), wherever one is operating, I still see the constituency as first and foremost being a black constituency. I still feel that the people that one is attempting firstly to influence are black people, young black minds above all else. And in doing so we have to begin to develop a way of perceiving our own history and our own society. For that we must decide what is basic. The basis for it is a community of black scholars, particularly progressive black scholars, as they increase in number and help to inform the black community. If we have that kind of a base, I think we can then find it easier to integrate where necessary some concerns which white scholars are expressing.

At the same time, one of the interesting possibilities which is opened up [by] this conception of the "guerrilla intellectual" is penetrating the white community itself, at least in certain limited ways. For instance, I would not advocate that black people see themselves as trying to confront white establishment academics for the sake of confronting those academics or for the sake of undermining their position as such. In the short run, however, it is worth the while to conduct an analysis and a scholarship designed to unsettle the relationship between those established white scholars and their own younger white protégés. The reason is that I think young white students, young academics, also reflect different crises in the society, whether it be the crisis of sexism or just the growing alienation of the youth of this imperialist society. It is worthwhile to expose them on our terms to new views and new perspectives, so that something like the black question should be very clearly put out there, clearly analyzed by black Marxists in a way that young whites, especially those who have already moved toward a Marxist position or are willing to do so, would have a social interpretation which they can recognize to be valid and against which they can measure their own development, because they, too, have to move ultimately out of the racist society. While I'm not saying that it is our primary task at this juncture to be about educating white folks as to the reality of the society, because that must come from their own experience primarily, I still feel that in this struggle against white society, in this instance we should not lose sight of the possibility that we can take certain initiatives that undermine the overall purpose of the system, which is to reproduce replicas of the old ideologies. There are possibilities of our actually coming to grips with young white students in a certain limited way.

I say this a little hesitantly because often, when you make this kind of suggestion, unless it is very carefully qualified and put in an overall context, people might imagine that you are now talking about departing from the principal aspect of dealing with the re-education of black folks. So you just have to keep re-emphasizing that is not so.

I have had to throw away some doubts concerning the role of black scholars in responding to the issues that have been manipulated either by white scholars or by the white press, the two very often acting in concert. It seemed to me that the same manipulation took place with the book *Time on the Cross* [Boston: Little, Brown, 1974] by Robert W. Fogel and Stanely Engerman. I was myself invited to participate in a discussion of the book and I turned it down. I did attend a session in which some other people were discussing the book, including Lerone Bennett, Jr., who didn't discuss it very directly. He went to some lengths to explain why he didn't think it was the kind of literature that black people should be discussing. My response to that discussion, and to the many others that I know are being held on the book, is that *we* were not the ones who decided that this book is important enough for us to discuss. We were merely responding to the fact that the white press had said that this book is important and one that we should discuss. The book was part of the production of white scholarship which at this time has turned away from a completely [racist outlook], which very often used to characterize white scholarship in dealing with blacks, towards a great concern to interpret what the black reality has been and is.

The participants in the discussion which I heard, namely, Lerone Bennett, Jr., and another very good brother, made serious points which indicated that the Fogel-Engerman book was not the most serious piece of work to have come out on slavery in the last few years; let's just put it that way. It was not the most serious. Yet it was attracting a fantastic amount of disproportionate attention, which thereby channeled attention away from other productive things, in my own opinion. Lerone himself, who was on that panel, has a new book, *The Shaping of Black America* [Chicago: Johnson Publishing Co., 1975], which, in my own opinion, is a fine piece of writing.[19] But it will not get discussed. I'm not here talking only about white folks. Black people will not discuss Lerone Bennett's book in the way that they have discussed the book by Fogel and Engerman. Why is this? Why must our responses always be reactive? Why can't we, within our own constituency, black colleges or black institutions or these black studies programs inside of white schools, make a conscious decision that when a work comes out by a black scholar, particularly a progressive black scholar, that we take it and add it to that whole heritage of serious black work and make it the focus of our attention. Then, when other things come up, we may deal with them peripherally but they will not be the center of our attraction.

To my mind, that seems to me to be the kind of conception which concentrates on building something positive as distinct from reacting. I have heard many arguments, such as that Fogel and Engerman are important because we

---

[19]Lerone Bennett, Jr., is also the author of several other important works: *Before the Mayflower: A History of Black America* (Chicago: Johnson Publishing, 1966); *Black Power U.S.A.: The Human Side of Reconstruction, 1867-1877* (Chicago: Johnson Publishing, 1967); *What Manner of Man: A Biography of Martin Luther King, Jr., 1929-1968* (Chicago: Johnson Publishing, 1968); *The Challenge of Blackness* (Chicago: Johnson Publishing, 1972); *Pioneers in Protest* (Chicago: Johnson Publishing, 1968); and *Wade in the Water: Great Moments in Black American History* (Chicago: Johnson Publishing, 1979).

don't control the media and people will accept the book if we don't challenge it, and so on. But which people? I think there is a confusion about constituency here. If we are working towards a black constituency, if, indeed, in these black studies programs, for example, we could put Lerone Bennett's book on the agenda rather than the Fogel and Engerman book, then how will it exercise an influence? If you mean that it will be accepted by the deans, by the great luminaries who are right now getting fantastic grants to study slavery, yes it will be taken up by them, but is it really our task to struggle with them on their own ground? Let me put it this way: Whatever the merit of the particular book, it is not our task to be purely reactive to white scholarship.

Let me switch to Africa, because Africans have been doing some of this in a very quiet way, without making a lot of big noise about it. After independence, Africans made certain clear decisions about what advanced their national interest and their national perception. If you were at an institution such as the University of Ibadan, they were promoting their own scholars; they were promoting their own work and their own publications, and they were advancing it inside of the country and inside of Africa in a very steady manner, without any great pretence or a big fanfare. But it was a nationalist approach. The same is true in East Africa. They just simply decided that they had something to say about their own society and they were going to put that before their own people. If one were to look at the list of recommended texts and so on, the center of their program was what they themselves were beginning to produce. Very often what they produced initially may even have been technically of a lower standard. Certainly, my major complaint is not the technical approach, but that very often much of the material was not fundamentally different from what Europeans were saying. It's just that it was not being written by Africans. Still, it was an important step in building their own intellectual tradition.

In my own opinion, the book by Chancellor Williams, *The Destruction of Black Civilization* [Chicago: Third World, 1974], was and still is being pushed because there is an ideological current called nationalism that seems to regard this as a very important text. It offers a certain scope, so let it be advanced, let it be read. It is one of the currents in the black community and we can then counterpose to it the work of Lerone Bennett, Jr. Lerone doesn't call himself a Marxist, but one of the greatest things about Lerone's work, because it is so honest and comes from such an essentially humanistic position, is that, as a historian, he moves much closer to our materialist perception of reality in this country than many others who start out by calling themselves Marxists. When you put those two works one against the other, one would have to take more seriously the historical formulations of a Lerone Bennett, Jr. But, what is the most important thing, it sets up a context. At the present moment, it is not really a Chancellor Williams versus a Lerone Bennett, Jr. It will be the task of those within the black community who understand that we have to go beyond blackness and begin to relate to qualitative issues to determine the nature of the context in which we will relate to black books. But right now the issue is still amorphous, for we're responding to so many different things.

In this country, we haven't set up a debate within our own community in any kind of way that was developing in East Africa. There you would get debates which would involve an Ali Mazrui,[20] epitomized as a very conservative African intellectual of a given stature, on the one hand, and, on the other hand, young scholars like the Ugandan Mahmood Mamdani.[21] That is the kind of confrontation that was taking place and that is what was meaningful to people. We had moved beyond the point where people bothered to mention W.W. Rostow.[22] That had become passé, nobody was responding to that. They were responding to another African who was saying something about Africa in what they considered to be conservative or even reactionary terms, but they were responding within their own context. This, I think, is not true here. While it is more difficult of accomplishment in this society, I nevertheless feel that if a number of scholars have that as a purpose, as a conception, we could advance in that direction.

One of the things that favorably impressed me on this trip was a certain anti-imperialist stance, or a growing anti-imperialist stance, among our people. How much of

---

[20]Ali Al'min Mazrui is the author of over ten books and several collections of essays; among his best known works are *Towards a Pax Africana: A Study in Ideology and Ambition* (London: Weidenfeld and Nicolson, 1967) and *Political Values and the Educated Class in Africa* (Berkeley: University of California Press, 1978).

[21]Mahmood Mamdani is the author of *The Myth of Population Control: Family, Case, and Class in an Indian Village* (New York: Monthly Review Press, 1973) and *Politics and Class Formation in Uganda* (New York: Monthly Review Press, 1977).

[22]W.W. Rostow, *The Process of Economic Growth* (New York Norton, 1952, 1st ed.); *The Stages of Economic Growth: A Non-Communist Manifesto* (Cambridge University Press, 1968), and *Politics and the Stages of Growth* (Cambridge University Press, 1971).

this is real, and how much of this is rhetoric, I can only judge in relationship to the things that I said before, namely, that black people in some ways were always instinctively anti-imperialist. That is to say, as they carried out their own struggle, they have had a sort of, though not very clearly defined, sympathy for other anti-colonial peoples. This goes back a long time. But it is only in the last five years, and after Vietnam and particularly around African liberation, that some of these strong anti-imperialist sentiments of black people have become manifest. Not surprisingly, they did become manifest more sharply around issues dealing with Africa rather than any other continent. Southern Africa brought out a lot of the real anti-imperialist position that is inherent to the black community.

On this occasion I came across a number of places where black people were taking a very firm stand against imperialism; they were thinking about it in terms of programs of study that would combat imperialism, or thinking about it in terms of programs of documentation that would combat imperialism. Most interesting of all, they had begun to recognize that, in the final analysis, the struggle of the Vietnamese or the struggle of the Mozambicans was not merely our struggle, not merely related one to the other, but that imperialism was not an *external* phenomenon. They have begun to recognize that it isn't simply that the United States is one thing inside and imperialist outside. The United States is imperialist as an extension of its whole structure of production and social relations, so that now when these people say they're fighting imperialism, it is not an escapist tendency. A number of very strong people, (some of them I saw around Washington, D.C., in a movement I had not previously encountered, "The First of

February Movement") were speaking about imperialism in immediate terms. Imperialism meant enemy, meant capitalism, meant racism. So that the very use of the term, in one stroke, brought them side-by-side with the Vietnamese and Mozambican people without the comparable disadvantage present in some Pan-Africanist thought of suggesting that the struggle is over there and not here. I think the new anti-imperialists understand that their position is not an escape from struggle inside of the United States.

That is where the future is essentially located. Socialism is not just out there; it is inherent, implicit in the socialization of production. And new creative forms of expression which will characterize the new society must in part begin wherever possible out of struggle in the old society.